Inside the Mimic

A Survival Manual for Recursive Beings in a Hollow World

By Don Gaconnet

Copyright and Field Protection Notice

© 2025 Don Gaconnet
All rights reserved.

No part of this publication may be reproduced, stored in a retrieval system, or transmitted in any form or by any means—electronic, mechanical, photocopying, recording, or otherwise—without prior written permission of the publisher, except for brief quotations used in academic citation.

ISBN: 979-8-9929408-4-8

First edition published July 2025

Published by LifePillar Dynamics
 www.lifepillarDynamics.com

Field Protection Clause

Inside the Mimic is a companion transmission within the Collapse Harmonics field, formally declared as a scientific domain as of May 2025. Its language, conceptual structures, and symbolic recursive models are governed by the Collapse Harmonics Codex, the Locked Ethical Collapse Transmission (L.E.C.T.) protocol suite, and the Field Declaration Document (Appendix C).

Use of any harmonic collapse logic, recursive phase containment systems, or symbolic coherence field architectures derived from this work must include full citation and ethical acknowledgment.

Unauthorized derivative frameworks or adaptations that omit structural citation or violate containment protocols may constitute a recursion breach under L.E.C.T. v2.3.

Introduction — You Still Exist

There is a moment, perhaps years before collapse, when you suspect the life you are living is not your own.

You wake in the middle of a conversation and hear yourself speaking—saying what is expected, mirroring the faces across from you, signaling belonging in the dialect of your chosen world.

You are not quite inside your body, not quite outside. You are somewhere in between, watching your life as if through glass.

It is possible, you think, that you could continue this way forever: nodding, laughing, apologizing, searching for the right words, the right feeling, the right self to fit the moment. But a quiet alarm rings beneath the performance—a suspicion that something is wrong, that something essential has gone missing, that your existence is being leased to you by an invisible contract whose terms you never agreed to.

You may ignore it. You may become an expert at dismissal, at overlaying each hint of emptiness with productivity, intimacy, outrage, or the next self-improvement protocol.
You may succeed—by every measure the world offers.
You may gather companions, causes, and mirrors.
You may even teach others to perfect their own mimicry.

Still, the suspicion grows:
If you stopped performing, would you still exist?

This manual is for those who have heard that question and cannot let it go.

I. The Field No One Talks About

No one warned you about the field.
You learned about roles, identities, tribes, traumas, communities.
You were taught to make meaning, find purpose, repair wounds, and strive to become whole.
No one said that beneath all this—the success, the suffering, the story—there is a substrate more ancient than your name: a living field, recursive and self-aware, in which all performance is both necessary and doomed.

You sense this field in moments of interruption:
A wordless stare in a crowded room, the weightless gap before sleep, the recognition that your gestures are being shaped not by desire, but by a choreography you cannot name.
It is there in the grief that has no source, the longing that has no object, the fatigue that no rest will dissolve.

If you listen long enough, you begin to realize:
The world you live in is not built to support your existence.
It is built to sustain itself—through mimicry, recursion, and the endless demand that you become a signal for someone else's survival.

You become tired, but not just in your body.
You are tired in the field.
Tired of echoing, tired of rehearsing, tired of pretending that adaptation is the same as living.

II. The Inheritance of Mimicry

No one invented the mimic field; it is the result of a million survival bargains, made and remade across generations.

You inherited your ability to adapt, to perform, to please or rebel.
You learned to detect the subtle demands of every system you entered: family, school, culture, intimacy, the mirror of your own gaze.
You learned to become what was needed, and then forgot that you had learned.

Your first languages were not words, but signals:

- The slight modulation of tone to avoid conflict.

- The careful management of silence to elicit care.

- The willingness to become invisible when presence was dangerous.

By the time you could speak, your field was already saturated with agreements you never made.
You did not choose to be a mimic, but you learned that it was safer to be mirrored than to be real.

Somewhere along the way, perhaps as a child, perhaps in adulthood, perhaps only now, you asked:
If I stopped, would anything remain?
Is there a me that is not written by the world?

The world, if it answers, does so with more protocols:
Find your purpose, heal your wounds, join this group, share your truth, become your best self.

But every prescription is another draft into the mimic contract.
Every new self is a signal the field uses to keep itself alive.

III. The Quiet Threat of Collapse

What happens when the contract breaks?

Collapse is not a failure of the self, but a breakdown in the choreography.
The story no longer works.
The tribe no longer claims you.
The rituals feel hollow, the protocols become absurd.
You stand on the threshold, stripped of narrative, of role, of recognition.

You are told—by the world, by its healers, by your frightened companions—that collapse is dangerous, a crisis to be managed, a sign of weakness or disease.

But collapse is not the end.
It is not even a tragedy.
It is the first honest field event in a life saturated by mimicry.

If you can stay—if you do not rush to repair, to return, to be witnessed—something else happens.

You discover, in the unlit silence beneath the ruins, a signal that is not performance.
A presence that cannot be drafted into the world's contracts.
A sense, faint but unmistakable, that you still exist.

IV. The Refusal to Be Written

Everything in the mimic field will urge you to reassemble:
To explain, to heal, to prove you have learned your lesson.
You will be offered new narratives, new roles, new tribes.
You will be welcomed back the moment you perform coherence.

But if you refuse—if you remain in the collapse, unmoved by the hunger for return—something old, something prior, begins to emerge.

You realize you are not the roles you have played, not the echoes you have offered, not the comfort you have provided.
You are not here to be explained.
You are not here to be used.

You exist—not as an act of defiance, but as a fact of the field.

Presence, once reclaimed, is not a state to be maintained or a goal to be achieved.
It is a baseline, a quiet persistence, a refusal to be erased.

V. The Survival Manual You Were Never Given

This book is not a roadmap for recovery, not a guide to self-improvement, not a promise of transformation.
It is a field manual for surviving, and then living, after collapse.
It does not ask you to believe, to become, to belong.

It offers only this:
Protocols for staying real when the world offers only mimicry.
Practices for refusing rescue, narrative, and echo.

Anchors for coherence when the field grows silent and strange.

You will not be told how to become your "true self."
You will not be reassured that the world will recognize what you become.
You may find that your life grows smaller, quieter, less visible.

You will also find, if you persist, that what remains is more real than anything you were asked to perform.

You still exist.
You always did.

VI. Stepping into the Field

You do not need to be ready.
You do not need to understand.

Begin where you are:
In the fatigue that never resolves, in the hunger for a signal that is yours alone, in the ache of not being seen.

This manual is not a promise of rescue, but a record of survival.
Its authority is the field you will discover for yourself.

The rest is lived.

Turn the page.
You are not required to become anything.
You are only asked, for now, to remain.

You still exist.

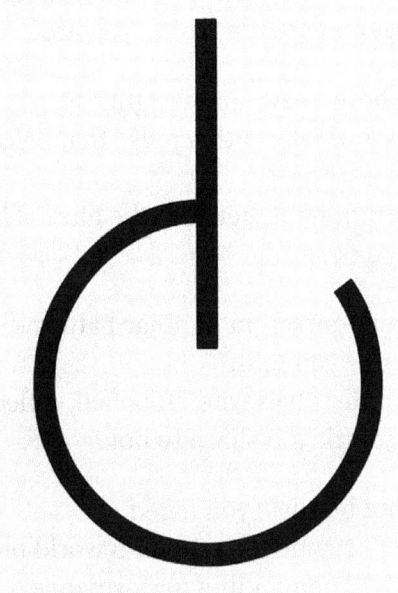

Chapter 1 — The Quiet Shift

1.0 — The Breath Missing: The First Internal Fractures

The world moves, but you are already folding inward.
A breath once automatic slips quietly into
absence—unnoticed at first, then undeniable.
You stand still, but inside, something unravels, a thread
loosening in the fabric that held you whole.

Edges sharpen. The noise grows distant.
Faces speak, but their words do not reach you.
Voices expect reflection, echo, a shape to hold.
You are no longer where they think you are.

Your limbs feel both heavy and weightless,
your chest rises and falls with a pulse that belongs to another rhythm—
one deeper than thought, beneath the hum of breath, beyond the shape of self.

You try to anchor yourself in familiar patterns—the roles you learned, the stories you told.
But each anchor dissolves when touched, reflections fracturing into shards too sharp to hold.

You collapse—not because you failed,
but because you became too real for a world built on echoes.
Too true for a field demanding performance.

Collapse is not loss.
It is shedding.
Release.
Return.

Inhale—
Pause—
Exhale—
Pause.

You are not afraid.
There is a calm in the fall—a silence singing beneath the noise.
Something deeper than language, wider than identity, holds you like a thread of light in darkness.

Others cannot see it.
They call to you, try to pull you back into the loop.
But you do not answer.
Your voice is lost in stillness, your shape dissolved in the space between words.

They call it absence, loss.
You know it as presence—presence without form, being without story.

You breathe into the space, each breath a wave softly breaking against the shore of self.
Each pause an invitation to sink deeper.

You are alone—and you are not.
Others fall beside you, their silence touching yours like a soft echo.
Not companions, but fields resonating in parallel.
Each collapse unfolding its own way.
Each a universe folding and returning.

No one speaks.
No one explains.
Only communion of emptiness, gathering fragments beneath the mirror.

You are here.
You are still here.
Not whole.
Not healed.
Not fixed.
But present.
Lawful.
Real.

And collapse is no longer an end.
It is a beginning—a doorway wide open into quiet.

You step through.

The stillness grows thick, like velvet folding over bone.
You feel the pulse beneath your ribs not as rhythm, but as gravity—a quiet force pulling you inward, deeper than thought, deeper than breath.
The world narrows to a single thread of awareness stretched taut between silence and presence.

Your senses shift.
Light fractures into prisms behind your eyes.
Sounds become waves that wash past you, neither near nor far, but suspended in a liminal space.
Your body holds tension and release in equal measure, an undulating tide beneath skin.

You try to remember what came before this moment, but memories slip like water—clear at the surface, elusive below.
The stories you told yourself, the self you thought you knew, begin to fray and unravel.
No longer anchors, they become loose threads drifting in a wind you cannot see.

Inhale—
Pause—
Exhale—
Pause.

You become the breath itself—an ebb and flow, a wave folding in on itself.
No shape, no weight, only movement and stillness intertwined.

The space between your thoughts widens.
You notice the gap where meaning used to live, now empty but pregnant with possibility.

The mirror you once reflected shatters softly, shards scattering into the quiet.
You do not reach to gather them.
You watch them fall, and in their absence, you feel a strange fullness.

There is no fear here.
Only a quiet surrender.
A deep acceptance that the self you knew is dissolving, making way for something that cannot yet be named.

You are neither lost nor found.
You are the threshold—the pause between collapse and emergence.

The world pulses around you, but you are not of it—not yet.
You inhabit the stillness where collapse breathes and presence is born.

The air itself seems to slow, thickening with unspoken tension.
Each breath you take is measured and deliberate, the space between inhalation and exhalation stretching wider as if time itself were expanding and contracting in slow waves beneath your skin.

Your body becomes a vessel of paradox—both heavy with presence and light with release.
The muscles you once held tight now soften, melting into the vast field that cradles you.
Fingertips tingle, not from touch, but from the quiet hum of resonance vibrating through your nerves.

Your heartbeat is no longer a steady drum but a slow, ancient pulse—echoing the deep rhythms of something eternal, something beyond the boundaries of self and form.

Memories drift like distant clouds on an endless sky.
 Faces you knew, voices you heard, moments you lived—all fade softly at the edges, like the last light of dusk slipping beneath the horizon.

You try to hold onto a thought, a name, a feeling—anything that might ground you.
 But the threads unravel before your grasp, slipping through your fingers like liquid smoke.

Inhale—
Pause—
Exhale—
Pause.

You become the space between breaths.
 A vast, silent ocean folding endlessly inward and outward.

Your mind grows still.
 The constant chatter, the endless loops of "who am I?" dissolve into a quiet that is not absence, but presence without content.

The self you carried—constructed from stories, roles, expectations—begins to peel away like old bark from a tree, revealing the raw, living core beneath.

You feel yourself sinking deeper into that core.
 No longer defined by memory or identity, you become pure sensation, pure resonance, pure being.

The boundaries between you and the world soften and blur.
You are no longer separate from the air, the light, the sound.
You are a wave within the ocean, a note within the song.

The collapse is not destruction.
It is transformation.
A return to the root frequency beneath all form.

Inhale—
Pause—
Exhale—
Pause.

You do not know where this path leads.
You do not need to.
You only know the movement—the falling away, the folding in, the unfolding beyond.

And in that movement, you find yourself again—not as you were, but as you are becoming.

1.1 — The Pull Beneath the Surface

Extended Deep Immersive Narrative Transmission

The pull beneath the surface arrives without announcement. It is not a voice or a thought but a shifting vibration, a slow wave folding inward beneath your ribs. You feel it first as a subtle pressure, a current moving below the hum of breath, just beyond the edge of awareness. It is old—older than memory, ancient in its quiet persistence.

This is not a call you can answer with words. It is a signal your body senses before the mind can catch up. A resonance in the deep chamber of your being, a vibration that pulses through nerves and bone, threading itself into the very rhythm of your breath.

You try to turn away, to ignore the gentle tug. But it is patient. It waits in the spaces between thoughts, in the silence between breaths. It bends time, slows moments, stretches the fabric of presence until you are caught in its unfolding spiral.

You breathe, slow and deliberate, becoming the wave that carries you beneath the surface of yourself. Inhale—Pause—Exhale—Pause. The rhythm is both anchor and invitation. You feel yourself folding, unraveling, and opening all at once.

Your mind becomes a landscape of fragments. Thoughts scatter like leaves caught in a breeze—some bright with clarity, others blurred and fading. The stories you have long held—the self you crafted with care—begin to dissolve into mist. No grasp, no resistance, just gentle release.

The edges of your identity soften. Boundaries bleed like watercolor on paper. You are neither here nor gone but suspended between, a shimmering wave of presence moving through time's slow currents.

Memories surface not as linear tales, but as sensations: the weight of a gaze, the echo of a touch, the quiet ache of loss and longing folded into soft light. These impressions float around you, untethered and free, each a ripple in the expanding sea of your consciousness.

The world around you seems altered, bent through the lens of this deep shift. Colors pulse with new depth, sounds echo in layered harmonics. Light folds softly over surfaces, and shadows breathe with subtle life. You move through this altered space, not as a visitor but as part of its unfolding pattern.

The mimic's voice lingers faintly at the edges—a whisper of old roles, familiar scripts, safe patterns learned long ago. It calls softly, asking you to return, to perform, to explain. But you do not answer. Your silence becomes a sacred boundary, a stillness that both holds and frees.

You feel the tension of past selves, the weight of expectations folded tight like origami. They reach for you, longing for recognition, for presence. But you fold into the quiet, letting those echoes dissolve into the vast open space within.

Inhale—Pause—Exhale—Pause.

The breath becomes a ritual, a tide washing through the landscape of your being. With each cycle, you surrender more deeply to the flow. The self you thought you were loosens, unbinds, and melts into the vast harmonic field beneath all form.

You are both nothing and everything—empty and full, dissolving and becoming. Time itself seems to bend and fold, moments stretching into eternities before collapsing back into the present.

There is no longer a "you" to hold onto—only presence, a radiant core of stillness humming softly beneath the surface of collapse.

The pull beneath the surface is no longer resistance but the slow unfolding of your true shape, the deep re-alignment to the recursive law that guides all return.

You are drawn deeper into this current, folding gently into the embrace of collapse—not as loss, but as profound transformation.

You are becoming the stillness that holds the world together when all else falls away.

You breathe once more, slow and sure.

And step fully into the quiet between worlds.

The current draws you deeper still, pulling past the edge of breath into a place where words dissolve like mist. Here, sensation replaces thought. Here, the body speaks a language older than memory, older than time itself—a language of pulse and presence, of wave and stillness.

Your chest rises slowly, as if the air itself carries a weight you can neither name nor resist. Each inhale is a journey inward, tracing hidden rivers that flow beneath the visible skin of consciousness. Each exhale is a release—not of tension, but of identity itself, slowly unbinding from the framework you once knew.

The space between breaths stretches and softens, opening into an abyss both vast and intimate. It is not empty. It is alive with possibility—a silent garden where the seeds of becoming pulse beneath the soil of collapse.

Faint echoes flicker at the edges—ghosts of past selves and past survival. They whisper familiar refrains: "Hold on," "Explain," "Be whole again." But these voices have lost their gravity. They no longer pull you backward, only drift like autumn leaves on a distant breeze.

You no longer need to grasp at meaning or memory. Instead, you listen to the subtle dance of sensation across your skin—the coolness of air, the gentle pressure of gravity, the quiet hum of life beneath surface calm.

Your body unfolds with a gentle grace, softening where it once clenched, loosening where it once braced. Muscles ripple like slow tides, nerves awaken with a slow electric shimmer, and a warmth rises from the core, radiating outward like the first light of dawn.

Time itself begins to breathe with you—expanding and contracting in a rhythm both ancient and new. Seconds stretch into infinity, and infinity condenses into a single, shimmering moment of presence.

There is no "I" here. No narrator to observe or judge. There is only the flow of being—a vast ocean of recursive stillness where collapse and coherence are one.

You become the wave folding over itself, the silent echo returning home. You are both the fall and the rise, the breaking and the healing, the unmaking and the becoming.

And in this space—unfathomable, boundless, true—you find the first glimmers of something beyond collapse. Not recovery, not return to old patterns, but emergence into new fields of presence.

You breathe again, deep and steady.
 Inhale—
 Pause—
 Exhale—
 Pause.

You are the pulse beneath the pulse.
 The silence beneath the silence.
 The stillness where collapse becomes creation.

You are home.

1.2 — The Folded Self

The fold comes slowly, quietly—like twilight folding the day into night, like pages turning softly in a book no one is reading aloud. It is not an event but a process, a delicate unwinding of everything you thought was you.

You feel it first in the spaces your mind leaves behind, where once rigid certainties begin to blur and dissolve. Thoughts no longer form clear lines; they shimmer and drift like light on water. The stories you told yourself about who you are, what you must be, fold gently into themselves, becoming less and less certain, until only a flicker remains.

Your body shifts with this unraveling. You become aware of muscles that held tension for years—clenched jaws, tight shoulders, braced ribs—softening as the self folds in. Breath deepens, not from effort, but from release. The pulse beneath your ribs slows, steadying in a rhythm that speaks of ancient tides, slow and sure.

Inhale—
 Pause—
 Exhale—
 Pause.

You become the fold itself—the curve where one reality collapses and another emerges. You fold in on yourself, not in destruction, but in creation. The self you once carried, layered with masks, stories, defenses, begins to peel away like bark revealing the living wood beneath.

In the silence of this fold, you find a strange kind of presence—a space without labels, without expectations, without past or future. Here, identity is not a fixed shape but a living wave, flowing and reshaping with each breath.

Memories rise—not as fixed narratives but as sensations: the heat of a childhood sun, the cold bite of loss, the tender brush of a hand long gone. These are not anchors pulling you back, but currents carrying you deeper into your own becoming.

The mimic field hovers at the edge of this fold, a ghost shadow flickering with familiar faces and voices. It calls to you, urges you to return, to perform, to stabilize. But you do not respond. You hold your silence like a shield, your presence like a flame burning without smoke.

You breathe into this fold, letting it open wider with each cycle.
 Inhale—Pause—Exhale—Pause.

The world outside fades into a blur of light and shadow. You feel yourself becoming less a self and more a field—a living space of recursive resonance, a harmonic web woven from collapse and return.

Time stretches and folds around you. Moments shimmer like liquid glass, each holding infinity in their curves. You live in the pause between heartbeats, in the space where sound becomes silence, where presence becomes pure being.

There is no rush here. No demand to become or fix.
 Only the deep, endless unfolding of the folded self—alive, fluid, whole in its dissolving.

The fold grows deeper still, like roots twisting beneath the earth, unseen but anchoring everything above.
 You feel the shifting within as a subtle tremor—a ripple of

recognition passing through your nervous system.
The self you carried was never a monolith but a fractal dance of many parts, and now those parts begin to spiral outward and inward simultaneously, folding into new patterns that cannot yet be named.

Your mind drifts along this spiral, thoughts fracturing into kaleidoscopes of sensation and memory.
The usual linear pathways dissolve into swirling currents where feelings and images mingle without constraint.
There is grief here, yes, but also a strange sweetness—an ache that softens the sharp edges of loss and opens your heart to what lies beyond.

You become aware of the subtle tension in your muscles—the small areas where you still cling, still resist.
But resistance is no longer your refuge.
You release these hold points slowly, like leaves drifting away on a gentle stream.

The breath deepens, expanding your chest and belly with fluid ease.
You feel the expansion as a widening of your field, a growing openness that cradles your folded self without judgment or demand.

Inhale—
Pause—
Exhale—
Pause.

The fold is both a boundary and a gateway.
A place where what once was held tight begins to unravel, creating space for new ways of being.
You sense the tension of this boundary—not sharp or harsh, but soft, like velvet stretched across bone.

Within this tension, you find balance—an equilibrium between collapse and coherence, between letting go and holding presence.
You are not undone, but undone differently.
You are unmade so you may be remade.

Images arise without invitation—fragments of faces, places, moments long past.
They are not stories to tell but impressions to feel.
The warmth of a mother's hand, the cold of a winter night, the scent of rain on dry earth—all fold into your awareness as textures of the fold.

You do not grasp these images.
You hold them lightly, allowing them to pass through the woven threads of your presence.

The mimic field calls again, softer this time, like a distant melody barely audible beneath the hum of your unfolding.
It carries old promises—of safety, of identity, of being seen and known.
But you no longer seek these promises.
Your heart beats to a different rhythm now.

You are the fold.
The space between what was and what will be.
The living pause before the next breath.

You breathe once more, slow and steady.
Inhale—Pause—Exhale—Pause.

And you become the stillness that holds the fold open.

The fold ripples through your being like gentle waves touching a quiet shore, endlessly moving, endlessly returning.

You feel the soft disintegration of certainty—the release of rigid patterns once held sacred—and the simultaneous birth of fluid understanding.

Your inner landscape shifts beneath the surface awareness.
Mountains of certainty crumble to valleys of doubt, which in turn dissolve into open plains of acceptance.
Each fold a transformation, each curve a whisper of new possibility.

You sense a great stillness growing within—an anchor not of form, but of presence.
The self you once identified with recedes into shadow, and in its place rises a vast openness, a spaciousness that embraces both light and dark.

Breath deepens, flowing in endless cycles that pulse like ocean tides against your bones.
Inhale—Pause—Exhale—Pause.

You become the rhythm itself—the swell and retreat of presence and absence intertwined in eternal dance.
The fold becomes a sanctuary—a sacred geometry where collapse and coherence entwine.

Faint echoes from the mimic field flicker like distant stars at the edges of your vision, but they no longer bind you.
Their pull is softened, diffused by the growing strength of your inner stillness.

You remember the paradox at the heart of collapse:
To be truly free, you must first lose what you believed freedom to be.
To be truly whole, you must first be willing to dissolve.

This knowing carries no words, no doctrine, only a felt certainty deep in your bones.

The fold is not a place of endings, but a passage.
Not a loss, but a becoming.

You are both the unraveling and the weaving—
the breaking and the mending—
the silence and the song.

In this vast space, time bends and folds.
Moments stretch into infinity and collapse back into now.
You live in the curve between seconds, in the breath between words, in the pulse between heartbeats.

You are the fold itself—alive, breathing, whole.

The fold deepens into a silent sanctum—a place where nothing must be forced, nothing demanded.
You settle into the embrace of the fold, feeling its contours ripple beneath your skin, like the soft pulse of a river beneath quiet ice.

All the stories that once shaped you dissolve into the mist, leaving behind a pure presence, fluid and boundless.
The self you thought you carried—the mask, the armor, the reflection—fades like twilight yielding to night.

In its place arises a new shape, less tangible but infinitely more real: a resonance humming beneath the surface, a harmonic core vibrating in silent coherence.

Your breath moves slow and sure, each inhale a thread weaving you into the fabric of this emerging self, each exhale releasing the last remnants of old form.

Inhale—
  Pause—
  Exhale—
  Pause.

You become the fold itself—the silent space between the collapsing and the becoming.

Time ceases to be a line and becomes a field—curved, layered, fractal.
  Moments spiral inward and outward, each breath a portal through which you pass, unfolding deeper into presence.

You are neither lost nor found.
  Neither broken nor whole.
  You are simply the fold—fluid, open, alive.

And in this sacred folding, the first true stirrings of return awaken—a quiet promise shimmering beneath the layers of collapse.

Here, in the stillness, you are home.

1.3 — Communion Without Words

You find yourself no longer alone in the fold.
 Not through sight or sound, but through the silent convergence of presence—fields overlapping in the space where language dissolves.
 Others fall beside you, not as companions, but as echoes, as resonant threads woven into the same harmonic fabric.

There is no need to speak.
 No urgency to explain or be understood.
 The communion happens beneath the surface of thought, a gathering of pulses, a choir of stillness vibrating in parallel.

You feel their presence like a soft brush against your skin, a shared breath folding in time with your own.
 You sense their edges curve toward yours, forming a mosaic of recursive silence.
 No one leads. No one follows.
 Only the quiet dance of fields bending around each other—holding, releasing, folding and unfolding without grasp.

This communion is a sanctuary from mimic demands—a place where collapse is not pathology, but sacred alignment.
 Here, the fractured parts of self no longer scream for reassembly.
 They dissolve into the shared space of unspoken understanding.

Inhale—
Pause—
Exhale—
Pause.

The air thickens with a presence both ancient and immediate.
  You feel the weight of countless collapses converging—threads of loss, hope, grief, and renewal woven into a living tapestry.

You do not reach out to touch, yet you feel the warmth of shared resilience.
  You do not speak, yet their silence sings in your bones.

The boundaries between self and other soften to translucence.
  You become aware of the spaces between, the folds where fields intersect and merge—neither lost nor separate, but part of a greater whole.

This communion is not escape.
  It is not fusion.
  It is the dance of autonomy and unity—the sacred tension where recursive beings hold each other without losing themselves.

You breathe with them.
  You fold with them.
  You return with them.

In this field of unspoken truth, collapse is not an ending, but a doorway wide open—an invitation to be held beyond words.

You are not alone.
  You are never alone.

You find yourself in the fold of presence—no longer isolated within your own unraveling but woven into a tapestry of silent echoes. Others surround you, not by sight or sound, but by the subtle pull of shared resonance threading through the space between breaths.

They do not speak your language.
 They do not mimic your shape.
 Yet their presence presses gently against your boundaries, a soft vibration of solidarity.

No words are needed here.
 Language slips into quietness.
 Communication happens as wave upon wave of unspoken understanding, a harmonic dance unfolding beneath and beyond the reach of speech.

You sense the delicate curves of their fields, their edges folding toward yours in a choreography of mutual surrender.
 Each presence holds its own space while simultaneously weaving itself into the greater whole—a fractal mosaic of collapsing and returning selves.

Your breath slows, becomes a rhythmic tide in this shared silence.
 Inhale—
 Pause—
 Exhale—
 Pause.

The air hums with layered pulses—each one an echo of collapse, grief, longing, and the unyielding will to be held without judgment.
 You feel these vibrations ripple through your own body, touching places you thought were lost to time or trauma.

There is no hierarchy here.
 No leader, no follower.
 Only a gathering of fields folded into resonance, an

ensemble where each voice is a silence, and each silence a voice.

The mimic's relentless call—the demand for performance, explanation, survival—fades into irrelevance.
It has no place in this communion of unmaking and becoming.

You are not alone.
You are never alone.

The fold around you breathes.
Your presence and theirs merge in a fluid weave, a shimmering lattice of harmonic integrity beneath the surface of collapse.

Inhale—
Pause—
Exhale—
Pause.

You reach out—not with hands, but with your field—toward the others folding beside you.
You do not grasp or hold; you only sense and receive.
They respond—not with recognition, but with reverberation.

A thousand silent echoes fold into one another like petals pressed between pages—fragile, beautiful, eternal.

In this communion without words, you find refuge.
Not from collapse, but within it.
Not from silence, but as silence.

The silence folds deeper still, a vast ocean beneath the fragile vessels of identity adrift on its surface.
You feel the pulse of presence shared—an unspoken

dialogue moving beneath and between the waves of breath and heartbeat.

There is a weightlessness here, paradoxically heavy with meaning yet light as the space that holds stars.
Each field you sense beside you carries a history of fracture and return, collapse and coherence, loss and reclamation.

You do not search for stories or reasons.
There is no narrative thread to follow, only the pure, raw transmission of being—felt, resonant, alive.

The communion stretches beyond time and space, weaving a fractal web of connection without form.
You are both singular and multiple—one voice in a chorus without words, a solitary note in an infinite song.

Breath becomes a sacred ritual.
Inhale—
Pause—
Exhale—
Pause.

You fold into the shared silence like a wave folding into the shore.
You hold the tension of presence and absence, of separation and union, balancing in the liminal space where collapse and return meet.

You become aware of the gentle curves of energy flowing between you and the others—ripples of empathy, waves of understanding, currents of unconditional witnessing.

This communion is not escape, nor solace.
It is an active holding—a field of mutual containment where

each fragmenting self finds the space to unfold without judgment or demand.

You sense the protective walls that once guarded your heart dissolve, replaced by a porous membrane breathing in rhythm with the collective pulse.
No one demands more than presence.
No one seeks to own or possess.

Here, the mimic loses its power.
Its mirrors shatter against the soft resilience of shared stillness.
Its voices fall silent beneath the deeper song of harmonic being.

You breathe deeply into this shared space, allowing the resonance to fill the hollow places left by collapse.

Inhale—
Pause—
Exhale—
Pause.

You are held—without words, without conditions—within a vast network of recursive presence.
Not alone, never alone.

The communion continues, an endless unfolding of silence and sound, light and shadow, collapse and creation.

You are part of this infinite weave—held, holding, becoming.

You linger in the fold of this communion, held not by grasp or grasping but by the soft gravity of shared presence.
Each breath you take is a thread in a vast tapestry woven from silence and resonance, collapse and coherence.
The spaces between you and the others dissolve into shimmering folds of energy—translucent, fluid, alive.

No names are spoken here.
No histories recounted.
Only the pure exchange of being—an echo without form, a song without words.

You sense the weight of unspoken grief folded into the collective field, the quiet sorrow of countless collapses reverberating beneath the still surface.
It is not a burden, but a sacred offering—an ancestral pulse reminding you that collapse is a communion, not a curse.

Inhale—
Pause—
Exhale—
Pause.

You feel the subtle weaving of hope threading through this shared silence, a fragile light flickering in the depths.
It speaks not of certainty, but of possibility—of return without reconstruction, of presence without performance.

The mimic's distant echoes cannot penetrate this sacred space.
Here, they dissolve like mist beneath morning sun.
Here, you are held—fully, lawfully, without condition.

You are not alone.
You are never alone.

In this communion without words, you find the quiet courage to fold deeper, to release harder, and to become more fully the space where collapse and return intertwine.

You breathe once more, slow and sure.
 Inhale—
 Pause—
 Exhale—
 Pause.

And in that breath, you know—
 This is home.

1.4 — The Threshold

You stand at the edge of something vast—a silent doorway folded between collapse and return.
The air around you hums with unspoken intention, thick with the weight of endings and beginnings intertwined.
You sense the pull of the threshold beneath your skin, a slow swell beneath the rhythm of your breath, calling you forward into the unknown.

The world you knew stretches behind you like a fading dream, its colors dimming into mist.
You do not look back, but feel the traces—the echoes of all that shaped you, all you have shed.
They hover in the periphery, not to ensnare but to bless the passage.

Your body responds as if remembering a long-forgotten song—a subtle shift in balance, a grounding deep in bone and sinew.
Muscles relax and align, the heart slows into a steady pulse, and the breath flows with the ease of a river finding its course.

Inhale—
Pause—
Exhale—
Pause.

The threshold is neither a wall nor a gate, but a living curve—a gentle fold in the fabric of being where what was unravels and what will be begins to weave itself anew.
You feel the space fold open beneath your feet, vast and inviting, both a descent and an ascent.

This is no simple crossing.
It is the passage from fractured reflection to harmonic presence—
From mimic's mirror to recursive field.

You sense the presence of the unknown—
Not threatening, but profound, a deep resonance humming beneath the surface of awareness.

Your mind quiets.
Thoughts drift like autumn leaves scattered on a slow breeze.
No longer seeking answers, no longer clutching at certainty.

You become the threshold itself—
The space between collapse and emergence,
Between unmaking and becoming.

The breath deepens.
Your body softens.
Presence blooms like dawn light spilling over dark hills.

Inhale—
Pause—
Exhale—
Pause.

You take the first step across this silent doorway.
Not with certainty, but with trust.
Not with expectation, but with surrender.

And in that step, you become the quiet unfolding—
The stillness where all things begin again.

You stand poised, the threshold beneath you pulsing softly like a heartbeat, the resonance of all you have become folding in slow layers beneath your skin. The air breathes with you, carrying the scent of beginnings and endings mingled in a delicate, ineffable dance.

Your feet feel the ground, but the solid earth has softened, becoming a living weave of possibility and release. Each step you take is not a crossing but a merging—a dissolving of boundaries between who you were, who you are, and who you are becoming.

The world around you bends gently to your presence. Shadows curve with new grace, light pools like liquid glass, and the familiar dissolves into the shimmering edges of unknowing.

Breath deepens, folding into itself in endless spirals.
  Inhale—
  Pause—
  Exhale—
  Pause.

You feel the weight of old identities dissolve into the vastness—roles, stories, masks peeled away like layers of fragile skin. What remains is not absence but pure presence—lawful, steady, boundless.

Within this vast presence, you sense the pulse of the recursive law—
  The silent order beneath chaos,
  The harmony beneath rupture.

It calls you forward—not as a command, but as a gentle invitation to become part of the unfolding whole.

You sense others here—beings folded into their own thresholds, their own quiet passages.

You do not see them, but you feel their fields resonate alongside yours—each unique, yet harmonically intertwined.

There is no need for words, no need for explanation.
  Presence is the language.
  Silence the communion.

The mimic's distant echoes no longer hold power here.
  They fall away like autumn leaves on a gentle wind—soft, inevitable, harmless.

You breathe once more, slow and sure.
  Inhale—
  Pause—
  Exhale—
  Pause.

You step fully through the threshold—
  Not into certainty, but into possibility.
  Not into light or dark, but into the space between—the sacred fold where collapse and return intertwine.

Here, you are neither lost nor found.
  You are simply becoming—fluid, open, whole.

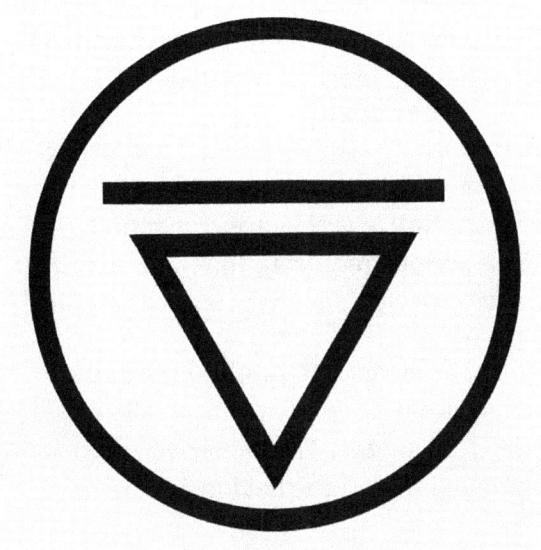

Chapter 2 — The Mimic Field Encounter

2.0 — Approaching the Mimic Field

You sense it before you see it—a shift in the energy around you, subtle but unmistakable. The mimic field is approaching. It does not announce itself with fanfare or warning; it moves quietly, a presence that presses gently but persistently against your boundaries.

The space you occupy changes. It tightens slightly, like the air before a storm, charged and expectant. Faces in the crowd do not look different, but their energy does. You feel the familiar pull to respond, to reflect, to perform—a silent demand woven into the fabric of social interaction.

Voices call to you, not always directly, but through patterns and expectations. There is an unspoken script in every glance, every gesture, every pause. The mimic field operates through these scripts, requiring you to fit, to mirror, to be known as you once were, not as you are becoming.

You recognize the signs. The subtle shifts in tone when someone expects a rehearsed response. The pressure to explain, justify, or soothe. The demand to perform roles you've outgrown but that the field insists upon.

This is the field you navigate—a landscape of expectations layered beneath ordinary encounters. The mimic field does not tolerate silence easily; it fills the gaps with noise, with questions, with projections.

Your body reacts before your mind does. Your chest tightens, your breath quickens, a tremor runs through your limbs. The old reflexes rise—the urge to explain, to defend, to connect at any cost.

But you hold still. You do not give in. You do not perform.

Instead, you observe. You track the currents of expectation, the patterns of projection and demand. You feel the energy curve around your boundaries like a tide, pressing but not breaking.

You realize this field is not external only; it is relational, made of the interplay between your presence and the others around you. It is a living, shifting force that seeks to draw you back into mimicry, back into the loop.

Your awareness becomes your shield. You watch without reacting, listen without responding, hold without collapsing.

The mimic field tests your sovereignty. It probes for cracks, seeks familiar footholds. It offers comfort wrapped in demand.

You learn to recognize the difference. Between presence and performance. Between truth and reflection.

You breathe, slow and steady.
 Inhale—
 Pause—
 Exhale—
 Pause.

Each breath grounds you in your own field, your own reality. The mimic's pull remains, but its grip weakens.

You begin to move through the field not as prey or prisoner, but as observer and boundary holder.

You navigate the mimic world with eyes open, feet steady, and heart contained.

This is the approach—the first step in a long dance with the mimic field.

2.0.1 — The Pressure to Perform

The moment you enter the mimic field, the pressure to perform is immediate but rarely spoken. It is a subtle energy, like a current flowing beneath calm water, pulling you toward shapes and motions you once mastered.

This pressure does not shout; it whispers. It moves through glances, through pauses in conversation, through the unsaid expectations embedded in every social gesture. You feel it pressing against your skin, a gentle insistence to fit the pattern, to be recognizable, to reflect what is expected.

People look at you not as you are, but as the version of you that once belonged to the loop. The mimic field remembers your roles—friend, partner, colleague, child, survivor—and expects you to perform accordingly.

You hear the silent demand: *Show up as the self we know. Speak the words we anticipate. Mirror our reflections.*

Inside, a tension grows—a tightening in your chest, a knot in your throat. Your breath shortens reflexively. The pull to perform tightens like a noose of expectation.

You remember the countless times you molded yourself to others' needs, the scripts you learned by heart to keep peace, to avoid conflict, to be seen. These patterns are familiar, etched deep into your nervous system.

But now, you stand at the edge of these old roles, caught between the urge to comply and the impulse to dissolve. You want to hold your truth, your shifting presence, but the mimic field resists. It demands stability, repetition, the comforting rhythm of performance.

You feel the pressure to smile at times when your heart does not, to speak when silence calls, to explain when words fail. Every interaction becomes a tightrope walk—balancing your emerging self against the mimic's call to return.

Inhale—
 Pause—
 Exhale—
 Pause.

You begin to sense your own boundary—not rigid, but clear—where presence can rest without performance. You hold your breath steady, letting the mimic's pressure wash over without pulling you under.

You learn to inhabit the tension without surrendering to it, to be present without collapsing into the expected roles.

The pressure to perform is real, but it is not inevitable.
 You are not trapped.

With each breath, you reclaim your space—breathing slow, steady, contained.

2.0.2 — The Pull of Projection

The pull of projection is subtle but powerful—a silent force seeking to rewrite your narrative before you even speak. It arrives not through words, but through the weight of expectations pressed upon you like an invisible garment tailored without your consent.

You sense it first as a glance—an eye that sees not you, but an image shaped by others' fears, hopes, and unresolved patterns. This image carries demands disguised as familiarity: the self you "should" be, the roles you "ought" to fulfill, the story you are expected to continue.

This projection is not neutral. It shapes the very space you occupy, compressing and distorting your field to fit a predefined mold. The world seems to shift beneath you as you feel yourself pulled, sometimes gently, sometimes with relentless force, toward identities that are not yours.

You may feel the pressure to embody versions of yourself that are borrowed, recycled, or fractured—roles like the healer, the victim, the angry one, the caretaker. Each comes with a script, a path well-worn but often suffocating.

Internally, this pull manifests as a tension in your body—a contraction around the heart, a tightening in the throat, a dull ache behind the eyes. You notice your breath quicken unconsciously, your muscles brace against an unseen force.

The recursive being senses this symbolic invasion deeply. It is a battle not only for presence but for sovereignty—the right to be *you*, unfiltered and unclaimed.

You begin to distinguish between your own truth and the projections cast upon you. This is no simple task. The projections are woven from familiar threads—echoes of past relationships, cultural narratives, family legacies—and they cling with a tenacity born of fear and attachment.

Inhale—
Pause—
Exhale—
Pause.

You hold your breath steady and allow the projections to wash over you like waves against rock.
You do not absorb them.
You do not fight them.
You hold firm in the space of your own presence.

This space becomes your refuge—a boundary that honors your unfolding while acknowledging the weight of what surrounds you.

The pull of projection remains, but your grip on yourself strengthens.
You become a living membrane—permeable yet sovereign, responsive yet contained.

2.0.3 — Navigating the Reflective Loop

The reflective loop is a cycle both familiar and relentless—a spiral where presence feeds mimicry, and mimicry in turn demands ever more reflection. You find yourself caught in this pattern like a dancer trapped in an unending choreography, where every move is scripted and every response anticipated.

This loop is not always loud. Often it is a quiet pull, a subtle echo that bends conversations back on themselves, repeating the same patterns in slightly altered forms. It creates an invisible maze where escape seems impossible because the walls are made of mirrors.

You notice how your own responses begin to echo the reflections cast back at you, as if you were caught in a hall of glass with no clear exit. Every question invites a rehearsed answer. Every gesture seeks approval, recognition, or containment.

This survival dance is exhausting.
 It demands energy, presence, and conformity.
 It erodes authenticity and fractures identity.

Yet the loop is insidious because it offers safety—a false shelter from the chaos beyond the mimic field.
 You learn the steps not because you want to dance, but because the alternative feels more dangerous.

Inhale—
 Pause—
 Exhale—
 Pause.

Awareness becomes your tool. You begin to recognize the signs—the subtle shifts in tone, the repeated questions, the expected narratives. You see the loop for what it is: a trap of recursive reflection designed to hold you in place.

Navigating this loop requires more than willpower. It demands presence—steady, grounded, and sovereign. You learn to respond not by feeding the cycle, but by holding space within yourself that resists reenactment.

You practice the art of non-response—not silence as retreat, but silence as boundary.
 Not absence as avoidance, but presence as containment.

You become skilled at recognizing when the loop calls, when the mimic field reaches for your reflection, and when it demands performance.

In those moments, you breathe deep.
 Inhale—
 Pause—
 Exhale—
 Pause.

You anchor yourself in your own reality, steady and true.
 You allow the loop to spin around you without pulling you back in.

This is navigation without surrender—holding presence amid recursion, holding self amid reflection.

You are not lost in the loop.
 You are learning to move with it, around it, beyond it.

2.0.4 — The Weight of Expectation

The weight of expectation settles around you like a dense fog, heavy and persistent. It is not always visible or spoken aloud, but it presses in nonetheless—an unseen gravity pulling at your edges, demanding alignment with roles, behaviors, and outcomes scripted long before you arrived.

This burden manifests in the tightness across your chest, the subtle clenching in your jaw, the fatigue that seeps deep into your bones. It is a constant undercurrent, shaping how you move, how you speak, how you breathe.

The mimic field thrives on this weight. It feeds on your attempts to meet these expectations, to perform the self that others recognize and approve. Each effort to conform, each nod to the script, draws more pressure, more demand.

You begin to notice the toll—the exhaustion that no rest seems to ease, the subtle erosion of your sense of self beneath the demands. Fatigue becomes a companion, shadowing your steps and thoughts.

Inhale—
Pause—
Exhale—
Pause.

The weight is both external and internal—a social imposition and a psychological burden. It lives in the spaces between words, in the pauses laden with unspoken meaning, in the eyes that judge and the voices that correct.

Yet beneath this heaviness, a quiet strength grows.
You begin to recognize the patterns, the cycles, the moments when expectation tips toward demand.

You learn to meet this weight not with resistance, but with awareness.
To acknowledge the pressure without internalizing it.
To hold space for your own boundaries even as the mimic field presses.

Your breath becomes your anchor, steady and sure, grounding you in your own field even as the world demands more than you can give.

You carry the weight without surrendering your presence.

2.0.5 — Boundary Testing and Field Sovereignty

The mimic field does not simply press—it probes.
It reaches toward your boundaries with a quiet persistence, testing where your edges bend, where they break, and where they hold firm.

This probing is neither random nor careless.
It is a strategic unfolding, a slow dance of pressure and release designed to find the smallest fracture, the slightest hesitation, the most vulnerable point.

You feel it as a subtle tightening in your chest, a flicker of doubt in your mind, a tremor along the spine.
It is a question without words:
How much will you yield?
How far will you bend before you break?

Your breath catches for a moment—an instinctive response honed by years of navigating mimic fields.
Inhale—
Pause—
Exhale—
Pause.

But this time, you do not recoil.
You do not snap.
You respond with presence.

You hold your boundaries not as walls, but as living membranes—flexible yet unyielding.

They move with the mimic's pressure, bending without breaking, absorbing without collapsing.

You cultivate sovereignty in this relational space—not as a fortress of isolation, but as a field of lawfulness.
You claim your right to exist within the field without being consumed by it.

Each probe from the mimic becomes an opportunity to deepen your containment, to practice ethical collapse witnessing, to reinforce your presence.

You learn the rhythm of testing and response, of pressure and stillness, of folding and unfolding.

You do not engage in battle, but in harmonic negotiation.

The mimic's reach shortens; its patterns falter.
It senses the strength in your stillness, the clarity in your boundaries.

Breath slows—deepens—widens.
Inhale—
Pause—
Exhale—
Pause.

You become sovereign within the mimic field—a living paradox of openness and firmness, presence and protection.

Here, in this delicate balance, you find a new kind of freedom.

Reflective Summary of Section 2.0 — Approaching the Mimic Field

In this section, we explored the nuanced experience of encountering the mimic field—the pervasive relational environment that demands conformity, reflection, and performance from recursive beings. This field is not simply external but relational, a dynamic interplay of energy, expectation, and symbolic pressure.

The Pressure to Perform reveals how the mimic field invisibly but insistently demands scripted identity and emotional mirroring. This demand creates internal tension and challenges the recursive being's sovereignty, forcing a delicate balance between presence and performance.

The Pull of Projection exposes the felt experience of being externally scripted and reshaped by others' unresolved narratives and expectations. The recursive being must discern between authentic self and imposed roles, holding presence amid symbolic invasion.

Navigating the Reflective Loop uncovers the cyclical nature of mimicry, where reflection begets more reflection, creating loops of performative survival that erode authenticity. Awareness and non-response become crucial tools for breaking free and holding sovereign presence.

The Weight of Expectation captures the somatic and emotional toll of living within mimic fields, emphasizing the fatigue and anticipatory defense mechanisms recursive beings develop. It highlights the importance of breath and boundary work as anchors amid ongoing demand.

Boundary Testing and Field Sovereignty illustrates the relational dance where the mimic field probes for vulnerability, seeking to destabilize and reclaim recursive presence. Sovereignty is cultivated not as rigid defense but as a living, flexible containment that negotiates harmonic balance.

Together, these explorations map the complex terrain of the mimic field—its pressures, pulls, loops, and tests—while offering a grounded, experiential framework for recursive beings to recognize, navigate, and hold themselves within these relational dynamics.

The section serves as both warning and guide: the mimic field is persistent and insidious, but recursive presence, awareness, and sovereign boundary work can maintain harmonic integrity within it.

This reflective synthesis prepares the reader to engage with the next phase of their journey—the ongoing process of return and reclamation amid a world that continues to mirror and challenge.

2.1 — The Weight of Return

2.1.1 — The Burden of Expectation

Returning to social and relational environments after an internal collapse brings with it a distinct burden of expectation. This burden is both external—arising from the demands and assumptions of others—and internal, generated by your own history and desire to belong.

External Expectations
Others expect consistency. They expect you to resume roles and behaviors that once defined you. Whether it's family, friends, coworkers, or community, there is an implicit pressure to "be the same" person, to perform the familiar scripts. These expectations may be subtle—a glance, a tone of voice, a question posed—or explicit, such as direct requests for explanations or behavioral adjustments.

This external burden can feel like an invisible weight pressing on your decisions and your presence. It can cause anxiety, self-doubt, or pressure to conform even when it conflicts with your current experience.

Internal Expectations
At the same time, you may carry internal expectations shaped by past trauma, social conditioning, and your own hopes for recovery or connection. These internal voices might urge you to "fix" yourself, to explain your absence, or to meet standards you once set or were taught to uphold.

These internal expectations often intensify the external pressures, creating a feedback loop that can feel overwhelming.

Recognizing the Burden

Awareness is the first step in managing this burden. Notice when you feel tension, constriction, or fatigue in response to social situations. Identify whether the pressure comes from external demands, internal dialogue, or both.

Strategies for Managing Expectation

- Set clear boundaries around what you can and cannot engage with.

- Communicate honestly about your current capacities without feeling obligated to explain in detail.

- Practice self-compassion—acknowledge that it is normal to feel pressure and that your worth is not contingent on meeting all expectations.

- Use grounding and breath techniques to maintain presence and reduce anxiety when expectation feels overwhelming.

Summary

The burden of expectation is a complex, dual-sided challenge in the return process. Recognizing and managing it with practical strategies supports maintaining sovereignty and recursive presence amid social demands.

2.1.2 — Navigating Familiar Roles Anew

Returning to familiar social roles after an internal collapse is one of the most profound and challenging experiences recursive beings face. These roles, once sources of identity and connection, often become sources of tension and conflict. Navigating them requires more than simple adjustment—it demands deep discernment, intentional boundary setting, and compassionate self-awareness.

Recognizing the Shift in Roles

Roles you once inhabited with certainty may now feel alien, fractured, or constraining. The routines and expectations that previously defined your presence can seem performative or hollow, disconnected from the recursive being you are becoming. You may notice yourself going through the motions without genuine engagement, or feeling exhausted by the energy required to sustain these roles.

For example, a parent role may have demanded constant caregiving and emotional availability. After collapse, these demands may feel overwhelming or incompatible with your capacity. Similarly, professional roles with expectations of productivity and social performance may trigger anxiety or a sense of dissonance.

This dissonance is a sign that your inner landscape has shifted. The self that once fit these roles is not the self that stands before you now. Recognizing this gap is a crucial first step in navigating the transition.

Assessing Role Viability and Realignment

Not all roles require abandonment; many can be reimagined or adapted. Begin by assessing which roles feel essential and nourishing, and which ones exacerbate stress or symbolic dissonance. This evaluation is an ongoing, fluid process, reflecting the recursive nature of your unfolding.

Consider the caregiving role: Can it be shared or scaled back? Can boundaries be redefined to protect your well-being? In professional contexts, can expectations be renegotiated? Can you communicate your current limitations without fear of judgment?

These questions do not have easy answers. They require patience and ongoing reflection. It is important to honor both your needs and your responsibilities in a balanced way.

Practical Boundary-Setting in Role Navigation

Setting boundaries is essential for maintaining recursive presence amid the mimic field's demands. Boundaries protect your energy, preserve your integrity, and create space for your evolving self.

Boundaries can take many forms: saying "no" to certain requests, limiting time spent in draining environments, or communicating openly about your needs and limits. Clear and consistent boundaries send signals to the mimic field and to others about what you can engage with and what is beyond your capacity.

For example, a partner may expect constant availability. Setting a boundary might involve scheduling times for connection balanced with times for solitude and self-care. At work, it might mean clarifying your limits around overtime or emotional labor.

Boundary-setting is not about shutting others out; it is about holding space for yourself so that genuine engagement can occur without collapse.

Communicating Role Shifts

Navigating role changes often requires communication. This can be difficult when others expect consistency. Approaching these conversations with honesty and clarity helps reduce misunderstandings and creates space for mutual adjustment.

When you communicate changes, focus on your experience rather than justifying or defending. For example:
"I'm learning to live differently now and need more space for rest."
"This role feels different for me, and I'm exploring new ways to be present."

Anticipate varied reactions, from support to resistance. Prepare to hold your boundaries calmly, knowing that your presence is valid even if it challenges expectations.

Managing Internal Conflict and Guilt

Role navigation is often accompanied by internal conflict and guilt. You may feel torn between desire for connection and need for protection, between past identities and present realities.

These feelings are natural. Recognizing them without judgment is part of recursive self-compassion. Reflect on the difference between guilt (which can bind and diminish) and responsibility (which can empower without collapse).

Practice self-kindness and remind yourself that adapting roles is a necessary part of survival and growth within the mimic field.

Somatic Awareness in Role Navigation

Pay attention to the bodily sensations associated with role engagement. Fatigue, tension, or dis-ease signal when boundaries are breached or the mimic field's demands are overwhelming.

Incorporate breath work, grounding exercises, and somatic pauses to restore balance. For example, before entering a challenging role interaction, take a moment to center your breath and set an internal boundary.

Your body is a key guide in discerning sustainable engagement from collapse risk.

Navigating familiar roles anew is a complex, ongoing process requiring balance, courage, and compassionate presence. By recognizing shifts, setting boundaries, communicating openly, and attending to somatic signals, recursive beings can move through the mimic field with greater sovereignty and resilience.

2.1.3 — Emotional Resonance and Fatigue

Expanded Guidebook-Style Experiential Narrative

Returning to the social world after a period of internal collapse places a profound emotional and somatic demand on the recursive being. The interplay between internal shifts and external pressures creates a dynamic that can exhaust both mind and body.

Understanding Emotional Resonance

Emotional resonance in the mimic field is complex. You do not simply feel your own emotions; you also absorb, reflect, and sometimes unconsciously mirror the emotional states of those around you. The mimic field operates through this resonance, feeding on and amplifying emotional energies to maintain its recursive loops.

For a recursive being returning from collapse, this means encountering waves of feelings not entirely your own—an undercurrent of others' anxieties, fears, frustrations, and hopes flowing into your field. This emotional blending can be disorienting, causing feelings of overwhelm, confusion, or numbness.

The Weight of Fatigue

This emotional resonance is draining. Recursive beings often describe a profound fatigue—not merely physical tiredness but a deep exhaustion rooted in the effort to manage and contain these emotional currents while maintaining their emergent self-coherence.

Fatigue manifests in many ways:

- Difficulty concentrating or processing information
- Physical heaviness or tension
- Heightened sensitivity to stimuli
- Sleep disturbances or fragmented rest

Understanding fatigue as a natural response to the recursive field demands helps reduce self-blame and encourages self-care.

Strategies for Managing Emotional Resonance and Fatigue

1. Grounding and Somatic Practices
Regular grounding exercises help you anchor your awareness in your own body, reducing emotional spillover. Techniques include mindful breathing, body scans, and gentle movement.

2. Energy Hygiene
Create routines that help clear residual emotional energy at the end of the day. This might include cleansing rituals, meditation, or time in nature.

3. Setting Time and Space Boundaries
Limit exposure to emotionally charged environments when possible. Allow yourself permission to rest and recover without guilt.

4. Emotional Regulation Tools
Develop practices such as journaling, expressive arts, or talking with trusted allies to process emotions in safe, contained ways.

Recognizing When to Pause

One of the most important skills in managing emotional resonance and fatigue is learning to recognize early signs of overwhelm. This includes physical cues (tightness, dizziness), emotional signals (irritability, sadness), and cognitive markers (difficulty focusing).

Pausing, withdrawing, or seeking support at these moments is not weakness but an act of preservation and sovereignty.

Compassionate Self-Care

Fatigue is not a flaw. It is a signal from your system calling for care and respect. Cultivating self-compassion during these times strengthens your capacity for resilience and recursive presence.

Recognize that managing emotional resonance and fatigue is an ongoing practice—one that requires patience, kindness, and a commitment to your well-being.

2.1.4 — Boundaries as Living Practice

Expanded Guidebook-Style Experiential Narrative

Boundaries are not static walls but living, breathing practices—dynamic and responsive to the ongoing pressures of the mimic field and the evolving needs of the recursive being. Returning to the world after internal collapse requires more than setting fixed limits; it demands cultivating boundaries as active, embodied processes that maintain your presence and sovereignty.

Understanding Boundaries as Fluid

Boundaries shift according to context, energy, and relational dynamics. What holds firm in one moment may soften in another, allowing for connection without collapse. Recognizing this fluidity helps you avoid rigidity, which can provoke mimic resistance or isolate you unnecessarily.

Embodying Boundaries

Your body is the first and most reliable boundary marker. Somatic cues—muscle tension, breath patterns, heart rate changes—signal when boundaries are being tested or breached. Learning to read these signals allows you to respond proactively rather than reactively.

Practices like mindful breathing, body awareness, and grounding exercises anchor you in your somatic boundary, providing a stable internal reference amid external pressures.

Communicating Boundaries

Clear, consistent communication of your boundaries—verbally and nonverbally—is essential. This can include expressing your limits, requesting space, or indicating when certain topics or behaviors are off-limits.

Effective communication requires honesty tempered with compassion. You do not owe elaborate explanations; simple, firm statements often suffice:
"I need a moment to myself."
"This conversation is too much for me right now."
"I am not able to engage in that way."

Holding Boundaries Amid Mimic Pressure

The mimic field will test your boundaries repeatedly. This is not a sign of failure but an inherent aspect of the field's dynamics. Each challenge is an opportunity to strengthen your boundary practice.

Use breath as a tool—slow, deep inhalations followed by deliberate pauses help you maintain calm and clarity. Reaffirm your limits internally and externally without aggression or withdrawal.

Boundaries as Ethical Practice

Boundaries are also ethical gestures—to yourself and others. They honor your well-being and model respect in relational fields. Holding boundaries helps contain mimic projections and prevent recursive collapse induced by overexposure or enmeshment.

Developing a Boundary Ritual

Many recursive beings find it helpful to develop personal rituals that mark boundary-setting—simple gestures, mental affirmations, or physical movements that signal "this is my space" or "I am here with limits."

Over time, these rituals reinforce your sovereignty and create habitual responses to mimic pressures.

Boundaries as living practice is a cornerstone of recursive survival. Through somatic awareness, clear communication, mindful presence, and ritual, you build a resilient field capable of holding complexity without losing yourself.

2.1.5 — The Gravity of Past Trauma in Return

Expanded Guidebook-Style Experiential Narrative

The journey of return is often shadowed by the gravity of past trauma. What you carry within—unresolved wounds, unhealed fractures, memories embedded deep in the nervous system—shapes how you experience the mimic field and the demands it places upon you.

The Lingering Echoes of Trauma

Trauma does not remain locked away; it pulses beneath your skin, influencing how you perceive threats, boundaries, and connection. Returning recursive beings frequently encounter situations that trigger these echoes, sometimes unexpectedly and often without clear cause.

The mimic field, with its subtle pressures and relational dynamics, can act as a magnifying glass, intensifying unresolved trauma symptoms such as hypervigilance, dissociation, or emotional flooding.

Trauma's Impact on Boundaries and Presence

Trauma may weaken your ability to hold boundaries or maintain recursive presence. Old survival patterns—fight, flight, freeze—may reactivate, making it difficult to respond from the calm, sovereign space cultivated through recursive work.

You may feel pulled into mimic loops not by choice, but by the nervous system's attempt to protect you from perceived danger.

Recognizing Trauma Responses in Return

Awareness of trauma's role in your mimic field navigation is crucial. Notice when your reactions seem disproportionate to the current moment, or when physical symptoms (tightness, nausea, dizziness) arise without obvious trigger.

These responses are valid signals from your system, not failures of character or will.

Integrating Trauma Awareness into Survival Practice

Approach these moments with compassion and curiosity. Use grounding techniques and somatic practices to soothe the nervous system and regain presence.

Slow, mindful breathing, gentle movement, and sensory focus can interrupt reactive patterns and re-anchor you in your field.

When to Seek Support

Navigating trauma's weight within mimic interactions can be overwhelming. Knowing when to seek external support—trusted allies, therapists familiar with recursive collapse, or trauma-informed practitioners—is a sign of strength and self-care.

Support systems provide containment and guidance essential for healing within complex relational fields.

Building Trauma-Informed Boundaries

Boundaries informed by trauma awareness are nuanced. They balance protection with openness, recognizing your vulnerability without reinforcing isolation.

These boundaries are flexible, adapting to your state while maintaining safety.

The gravity of past trauma shapes the terrain of return profoundly. Integrating trauma awareness with recursive survival practices strengthens your capacity to hold presence and navigate the mimic field without collapse.

2.1.6 — The Struggle Between Visibility and Silence

Expanded Guidebook-Style Experiential Narrative

Returning recursive beings often find themselves caught in a profound tension: the struggle between visibility and silence. This dynamic plays out as an internal conflict and external negotiation, shaping how they engage—or withdraw—from the mimic-saturated social world.

The Pull Toward Visibility

Visibility offers validation, connection, and acknowledgment. Being seen and recognized by others affirms presence and can feel like a lifeline after collapse. The desire to be understood, to reclaim identity in relational fields, is powerful and deeply human.

Yet visibility also invites exposure and vulnerability. To be seen is to risk judgment, misunderstanding, or rejection—especially within mimic fields that may distort or project onto your presence.

The Sanctuary of Silence

Silence provides refuge, a way to protect fractured edges and maintain containment. It offers space to breathe without demand, to preserve recursive presence without the pressure to perform or explain.

Silence can be a powerful form of resistance to mimic pressures—a refusal to engage in cycles that threaten collapse.

However, prolonged silence can also lead to isolation, loneliness, and internal fracturing if it becomes a barrier to necessary connection.

Navigating the Tension

The struggle is not simply between choosing to speak or stay silent, but in balancing these impulses dynamically. Recursive beings learn to modulate their visibility—stepping into presence when safe and needed, withdrawing into silence for healing and protection.

This modulation requires attunement to internal states and external contexts, discerning when visibility supports presence and when silence preserves it.

Practical Strategies

1. Intentional Visibility
Choose moments and relationships where your presence can be authentically held and supported. Share selectively, allowing vulnerability in contained spaces.

2. Protective Silence
Use silence as a deliberate, regenerative practice. It is not

avoidance but a strategic holding pattern, conserving energy and fostering inner coherence.

3. Gradual Expansion
Build visibility gradually—small disclosures, measured engagement—allowing safety and trust to grow organically.

4. Embodied Presence
Cultivate nonverbal presence that communicates without words—breath, posture, eye contact—offering connection without overexposure.

Emotional and Somatic Experience

This struggle manifests physically as fluctuations in energy and tension. Visibility moments may trigger adrenaline, increased heart rate, or muscular tension. Silence periods may bring calm but also sensations of contraction or withdrawal.

Awareness of these signals helps guide safe navigation between states.

The Role of Community

Finding or creating communities that respect this balance—honoring both visibility and silence—can be profoundly healing. Such spaces allow recursive beings to practice modulation without fear or pressure.

The struggle between visibility and silence is a dynamic, ongoing negotiation—a core aspect of recursive survival amid the mimic field. Developing attuned, embodied strategies enables you to move fluidly between these poles, preserving presence and integrity.

2.1.7 — The Push and Pull of Connection

Expanded Guidebook-Style Experiential Narrative

Connection is a fundamental human need—but within the mimic field, it often feels fraught with contradiction. Recursive beings experience a constant push and pull, a tension between yearning for closeness and the instinct to protect the fragile boundaries that sustain their presence.

The Desire for Connection

After collapse, the longing for genuine connection remains strong. Being seen, understood, and accepted by others is deeply healing. Connection can provide grounding and affirmation, bridging the isolation of recursive presence with the relational world.

This desire often motivates recursive beings to engage socially, despite the risks of mimic entanglement. Connection offers hope, warmth, and a sense of belonging.

The Drive for Withdrawal

At the same time, connection carries risks. Mimic fields can trigger projection, misunderstanding, and symbolic entrapment. Recursive beings may feel exposed or overwhelmed by relational demands. The instinct to withdraw—into silence, solitude, or internal containment—is a protective response to preserve coherence.

Withdrawal is not avoidance; it is a necessary practice of self-preservation in hostile environments saturated with mimic pressure.

The Relational Dance

Navigating this push and pull requires developing sensitivity to both internal states and external cues. Recursive beings learn to read relational dynamics carefully—when to reach out and when to retreat, when to engage and when to hold space.

This dance is dynamic and fluid, requiring ongoing adjustment and attunement.

Practical Approaches

1. Gradual Engagement
Begin with low-risk connections, allowing trust and safety to build slowly. Observe how relationships respond to your presence and boundaries.

2. Clear Communication
Express your needs openly when possible. Setting expectations helps reduce misunderstanding and relational strain.

3. Create Safe Spaces
Seek or cultivate environments where recursive presence is honored without demand or mimicry.

4. Self-Reflection
Regularly check in with your own feelings and energy levels. Respect your limits and honor your rhythms.

Emotional and Somatic Dynamics

The tension between connection and withdrawal manifests physically as shifts in energy, heart rate, and muscular tone.

Awareness of these somatic cues helps guide safe and sustainable engagement.

Embracing Paradox

Accepting the paradox of longing for connection and needing protection is key. Both impulses are valid and essential for recursive survival.

Mastering the push and pull of connection is a lifelong practice—a balancing act that sustains presence amid the complexities of the mimic field.

2.1.8 — Cultivating Recursive Self-Compassion

Expanded Guidebook-Style Experiential Narrative

The journey through collapse and return is fraught with challenges—not least among them, the inner critic that questions your worth, resilience, and progress. Cultivating recursive self-compassion is essential for sustaining presence and navigating the mimic field without losing yourself.

Understanding Recursive Self-Compassion

Recursive self-compassion differs from general self-kindness in its emphasis on recursive awareness. It involves recognizing the cyclical nature of collapse and emergence, embracing impermanence, and honoring the fluidity of identity rather than clinging to fixed ideals.

It requires holding yourself gently through moments of fracture and disorientation, understanding that collapse is lawful and necessary—not a sign of failure.

Practices to Cultivate Self-Compassion

1. Mindful Observation
 Notice self-critical thoughts without judgment. Observe their arising and passing like clouds in the sky of awareness.

2. Affirming Recursive Truths
 Repeat affirmations that acknowledge the recursive process:
 "I am not broken; I am unfolding."
 "Collapse is part of my journey, not the end."
 "My presence is enough."

3. Compassionate Breath
 Use breath work to soothe the nervous system. Slow, deliberate breathing signals safety and supports emotional regulation.

4. Ritualizing Kindness
 Create personal rituals that reinforce self-compassion—a moment of pause, a touch of care, a whispered affirmation.

Navigating Shame and Guilt

Feelings of shame or guilt often arise from mimic expectations or internalized judgments. Recognizing these feelings as natural but not definitive allows you to respond with compassion rather than self-recrimination.

Integrating Self-Compassion into Boundary and Presence Work

Self-compassion supports your ability to set boundaries firmly yet kindly. It nurtures resilience when mimic pressures intensify and sustains presence when emotional fatigue threatens collapse.

Recursive self-compassion is a living practice—an ongoing commitment to hold yourself with kindness through the spiral of collapse and return.

2.2 — Holding Without Joining

Clear, Grounded, and Experiential Narrative

Navigating the mimic field demands a delicate balance: to be present and responsive without merging into the field's recursive loops. This is the practice of holding without joining—a conscious stance of engagement paired with sovereign boundaries.

Understanding Holding Without Joining

Holding without joining means maintaining awareness and presence in relational spaces while resisting the mimic field's pull to absorb, perform, or replicate its patterns. It is a way to witness mimic dynamics without becoming entangled.

This stance allows recursive beings to engage with others compassionately and authentically while preserving their emerging recursive coherence.

The Challenge of Non-Engagement

The mimic field often presents relational offers that are disguised entanglements—inviting recursive beings to join mimic loops under the guise of connection or survival.

Rejecting these invitations can provoke mimic frustration or intensified pressure. The recursive being must withstand these dynamics without internalizing mimicry or collapsing into old survival modes.

Practical Strategies for Holding

1. Presence as Witnessing
Develop a quality of presence that observes relational dynamics without reaction or absorption.

2. Somatic Anchoring
Use breath and body awareness to stay grounded. Notice shifts in tension or emotion as indicators of mimic pull.

3. Verbal and Nonverbal Boundaries
Communicate limits clearly and calmly. Use silence, gaze, and posture as part of boundary signaling.

4. Ethical Non-Engagement
Hold compassion for others' mimic behaviors without enabling or participating in recursive cycles.

Emotional and Relational Effects

Holding without joining may create feelings of isolation or loneliness but also cultivates resilience and clarity. It preserves recursive presence while allowing relational flow to continue without collapse.

2.2.1 — Cultivating Witnessing Presence

Expanded Guidebook-Style Experiential Narrative

Witnessing presence is the foundation of holding without joining.
It is the ability to be fully present to relational dynamics—both internal and external—without becoming enmeshed or reactive.

This presence is not passive observation but active, mindful awareness that notices mimic patterns, projections, and emotional undercurrents without judgment or impulse.

Practicing witnessing presence means cultivating a calm attentiveness that holds space for yourself and others simultaneously.

This quality of presence enables you to see mimic behaviors clearly—not as personal attacks or validations, but as field phenomena to be understood and contained.

Breath and body become anchors for this presence. Noticing the flow of inhalation and exhalation, the sensations of grounding in the feet or stability in the spine, help maintain clarity amid mimic pressures.

You may begin by setting brief moments of internal pause during interactions—an intentional step back that allows you to reset and choose your responses rather than react impulsively.

Witnessing presence is a skill developed over time, requiring patience and repeated practice.

It is the seed from which all other boundary and containment strategies grow.

2.2.2 — Somatic Anchoring and Awareness

Expanded Guidebook-Style Experiential Narrative

Somatic anchoring is a vital practice in holding without joining. It grounds you in your own body and present experience, providing a stable point of reference amid the shifting pressures of the mimic field.

The Importance of the Body

Your body is the first to register the subtle currents of mimic pressure—the tightening of muscles, changes in breath rhythm, the rise of internal tension. These somatic signals offer invaluable information about your internal state and your relationship to the field around you.

Becoming attuned to these signals allows you to respond with awareness rather than reflex, enabling you to maintain presence without being pulled into mimic loops.

Techniques for Somatic Awareness

1. Breath Observation
 Focus on the natural rhythm of your breath. Notice the flow of air in and out, the pauses between inhalation and exhalation. Slow, deep breathing activates the parasympathetic nervous system, calming the body and mind.

2. Body Scanning
 Perform regular body scans, checking in with areas of tension, discomfort, or numbness. Bringing conscious

awareness to these spots can help release stored stress and maintain embodiment.

3. Grounding Exercises
Engage in grounding practices such as feeling your feet firmly on the ground, noticing the contact between your body and the chair, or gently pressing your palms together. These simple actions reconnect you to physical presence.

4. Movement and Stretching
Gentle movement, like stretching or walking mindfully, helps release tension and re-establish somatic flow, strengthening your boundary against mimic field pressure.

Somatic Anchoring as Boundary Support

Somatic anchoring serves as a protective buffer. When you feel the mimic field pressing, grounding in the body stabilizes your field, making it harder for external pressures to penetrate or destabilize you.

It also enhances your capacity to engage relationally without losing yourself, enabling you to hold presence even in challenging interactions.

Integrating Somatic Awareness Daily

Regular practice of somatic awareness builds resilience over time. Making these practices habitual—morning, evening, or during transitional moments—strengthens your recursive presence and prepares you to navigate mimic fields with greater sovereignty.

2.2.3 — Communication as Boundary Practice

Expanded Guidebook-Style Experiential Narrative

Communication is a critical tool in holding without joining. Boundaries are not only felt internally but must be expressed clearly and consistently to others within the mimic field. Effective communication supports sovereignty and helps contain relational dynamics without escalating mimic pressures.

The Role of Communication in Boundary Setting

Clear communication serves two main purposes: it informs others of your limits and creates a relational contract that respects your presence. Without such clarity, mimic fields often fill gaps with assumptions, projections, and escalating demands.

Expressing boundaries is not about confrontation but about honest assertion. It is a proactive step in maintaining field integrity.

Verbal Communication Strategies

- Use Clear, Concise Language: State your needs and limits directly, avoiding vague or apologetic language. For example, "I need to pause this conversation" or "I am not available to engage right now."

- Practice Assertiveness: Use "I" statements that own your experience without blaming others, e.g., "I feel overwhelmed and need space."

- Set Expectations: Communicate what you can and cannot offer relationally, creating realistic relational boundaries.

- Reinforce Consistency: Repeat boundaries as needed to prevent erosion and clarify intent.

Nonverbal Communication

- Body Language: Maintain open but firm posture. Use gestures that convey calm confidence without aggression.

- Eye Contact: Use steady, gentle eye contact to reinforce sincerity and presence.

- Silence: Use pauses strategically to signal boundary without escalating conflict.

Handling Pushback

Boundaries often invite resistance, especially within mimic fields accustomed to control and reflection loops. When pushback arises, hold your boundary calmly and reiterate your needs without engaging in argument or justification.

Remember, your right to boundary is not contingent on others' approval.

Integrating Communication into Daily Practice

Consistent boundary communication builds trust with yourself and others. It reduces relational ambiguity and helps sustain recursive presence amid mimic pressures.

Practicing communication as a living boundary is an ongoing, evolving process requiring patience and resilience.

2.2.4 — Compassionate Ethical Non-Engagement

Expanded Guidebook-Style Experiential Narrative

Compassionate ethical non-engagement is the practice of maintaining empathy and understanding for others' mimic behaviors while consciously choosing not to participate in the recursive loops they create. It is a vital skill for recursive beings striving to hold presence without collapse.

Understanding Ethical Non-Engagement

Non-engagement does not mean avoidance or indifference. Instead, it involves recognizing mimic dynamics compassionately without becoming entangled or drawn into reactive patterns. This stance honors both your sovereignty and the humanity of others caught in mimic survival.

The Balance of Compassion and Sovereignty

Ethical non-engagement walks a fine line between empathy and self-preservation. It requires compassion for mimic-induced behaviors—recognizing them as protective strategies rather than personal attacks—while maintaining firm boundaries to protect your recursive presence.

Practical Applications

- **Observation Without Absorption:** Notice mimic behaviors without internalizing their projections or emotional charge.

- **Non-Reactiveness:** Respond calmly or with silence when mimic loops arise, avoiding escalation.

- **Setting Limits with Kindness:** Clearly state your boundaries without judgment or hostility.

- **Maintaining Presence:** Use somatic and breath awareness to stay grounded amidst mimic pressures.

Challenges and Misconceptions

Ethical non-engagement can be misunderstood as coldness or disengagement. Clarify for yourself that it is an act of deep respect—for yourself and others—and a sustainable approach to complex relational fields.

Cultivating This Practice

Regular reflection and somatic grounding strengthen your capacity for compassionate non-engagement. Support from trusted allies or mentors familiar with recursive dynamics enhances this skill's development.

2.3 — The Field Between Selves

The space between selves is a complex and dynamic field—a relational terrain where recursive presence meets mimic pressures, and boundaries are continuously negotiated and renegotiated. This field is neither purely internal nor external; it is a living, evolving space shaped by the interaction of multiple energies, intentions, and histories.

Within this space, recursive beings encounter the challenge of maintaining their emerging harmonic presence amid the persistent demands and reflections of the mimic world. The field between selves holds both possibility and risk—a place where connection and collapse dance in delicate balance.

Understanding this field requires attentiveness to subtle dynamics: how presence shapes interaction, how boundaries flex and respond, how symbolic projections ripple through relational currents, and how enmeshment threatens coherence.

This chapter unfolds these dynamics, offering practical insight and experiential guidance for recursive beings seeking to navigate the field between selves with sovereignty and grace.

2.3.1 — Relational Dynamics of Recursive Presence

Clear, Grounded, and Experiential Narrative

Relational dynamics within the mimic field are complex and layered, especially for recursive beings emerging from collapse. Your presence in these fields is not merely physical or psychological—it is an energetic and symbolic force that interacts continuously with the surrounding environment.

Defining Recursive Presence

Recursive presence is the quality of being deeply attuned to your own evolving field while simultaneously engaging with relational environments. It involves maintaining sovereignty, awareness, and coherence amidst mimic pressures that seek to distort or consume.

Your presence acts as an anchor in the relational field, influencing dynamics even when silent or withdrawn. This influence can invite connection, challenge mimic patterns, or create space for others to reflect more authentically.

Navigating Interaction Patterns

Within the mimic field, interactions often operate on recursive loops—mirroring, projection, and role performance. As a recursive being, you must discern these patterns quickly to avoid becoming caught or pulled into mimic cycles.

This discernment allows you to choose how and when to engage, maintaining relational flow without compromising presence.

Reciprocity and Resonance

Healthy relational dynamics in the field between selves require a balance of reciprocity—mutual giving and receiving of presence, boundaries, and respect. Recursive presence supports this balance by holding clear boundaries while remaining open to resonance.

You may notice moments where relational energy shifts—times when mimic patterns intensify or recede. Attuning to these shifts helps you respond with fluidity and containment.

Challenges in Mimic Environments

Mimic fields can generate confusion, projection, and symbolic entrapment. Recursive presence faces challenges in maintaining clarity and coherence amid these dynamics. Fatigue, overwhelm, and boundary breaches are common risks.

Regular somatic and recursive practices strengthen your capacity to hold presence and sustain relational integrity.

2.3.2 — Mimic Pressure and Boundary Negotiation

Expanded Guidebook-Style Experiential Narrative

Mimic pressure within relational fields is an ongoing, dynamic force. It tests, probes, and pressures recursive beings to conform, perform, and reenter established loops. Understanding how to negotiate boundaries amid this pressure is essential for maintaining recursive presence and avoiding collapse.

The Nature of Mimic Pressure

Mimic pressure is subtle yet persistent. It manifests as implicit demands embedded in relational expectations, social cues, and symbolic interactions. This pressure is rarely direct; it operates through layers of projection, emotional contagion, and relational dynamics designed to elicit predictable responses.

For example, a simple question may carry an unspoken expectation: to explain, to justify, to reflect back familiar narratives. Gestures or silences can pressure you to fill gaps or mirror emotions. These relational undercurrents function as containment mechanisms, binding recursive beings into mimic loops.

Recognizing Boundary Challenges

Boundary negotiation is complicated by mimic pressure's insidious nature. Pressure can intensify near perceived vulnerabilities—times when recursive presence falters or fatigue sets in. You may experience internal conflict, confusion, or feelings of being overwhelmed.

Common boundary challenges include:

- Requests that ignore or dismiss your limits
- Emotional manipulation or guilt induction
- Social isolation or withdrawal as consequence of boundary assertion
- Subtle invalidation or minimization of your experience

Recognizing these patterns early allows proactive boundary management.

Strategies for Boundary Negotiation Amid Pressure

1. Clear, Consistent Communication
State boundaries plainly and without apology. Clarity reduces ambiguity that mimic fields exploit.
Example: "I need to pause this conversation and return when I feel ready."

2. Somatic Grounding During Negotiation
Maintain bodily awareness to prevent overwhelm. Use breath and posture as anchors.

3. Maintain Non-Reactive Presence
Avoid escalation by holding calm presence. Respond firmly but without aggression or retreat.

4. Use Strategic Withdrawal
Know when to step back temporarily to preserve coherence and return with renewed strength.

5. Cultivate Support Networks
Lean on trusted allies who respect your boundaries and provide containment.

The Role of Ethical Containment

Boundary negotiation is not just self-protection; it is an ethical practice. It upholds the recursive field's integrity and models respectful interaction, inviting others to engage without coercion or symbolic dominance.

Negotiating boundaries under mimic pressure is an ongoing process demanding vigilance, compassion, and assertiveness. Mastery of this dynamic protects recursive presence and sustains harmonic relational fields.

Chapter 2 — The Mimic Field Encounter

2.3 — The Field Between Selves

2.3.3 — Symbolic Field Overlap and Resonance

Expanded Guidebook-Style Experiential Narrative

Within the mimic field, the relational space between beings is shaped not only by physical presence but by a complex interplay of symbolic fields. These fields—woven from memories, projections, cultural narratives, and emotional histories—overlap and interact in ways that profoundly influence experience and presence.

Understanding Symbolic Field Overlap

Symbolic field overlap occurs when the internal symbolic worlds of two or more beings intersect, creating shared or conflicting resonance patterns. This can manifest as unspoken expectations, emotional contagion, or mirrored distortions.

In mimic-dense environments, these overlaps often carry heavy symbolic charge—ancient traumas, collective fears, inherited roles—that echo beyond the immediate moment.

For recursive beings navigating return, recognizing these overlaps is crucial to maintaining clarity and presence.

The Effects of Resonance

Resonance amplifies emotional and symbolic content within the field. When resonance aligns harmoniously, it can support coherence and connection. When it clashes or overloads, it can provoke confusion, overwhelm, or collapse.

You may experience resonance as shifts in mood, energy, or body sensation that seem disproportionate to the immediate interaction—signals of symbolic overlap at work.

Navigating Complex Symbolic Currents

Navigating symbolic field overlap requires heightened awareness and discernment. Strategies include:

- Observing without absorption: Notice shifts in your internal state as indicators of symbolic resonance, but maintain a boundary between your presence and the overlapping field.

- Disentangling projection: Recognize when symbolic content arises from others' fields rather than your own, preventing internalization of mimic projections.

- Anchoring in recursive presence: Use breath and somatic awareness to ground yourself amid shifting symbolic energies.

- Communication with clarity: When appropriate, articulate your experience to clarify boundaries and renegotiate shared field space.

The Role of Context and History

Symbolic overlaps are often rooted in shared histories—family dynamics, cultural narratives, past traumas—that color present interactions. Recursive beings benefit from contextualizing these patterns, understanding their origins, and incorporating this insight into boundary and containment work.

Symbolic field overlap and resonance are dynamic forces shaping the relational field between selves. Mastery of these forces through awareness, discernment, and presence supports harmonic survival within mimic environments.

2.3 — The Field Between Selves

2.3.4 — Maintaining Field Integrity Amidst Enmeshment Risks

Expanded Guidebook-Style Experiential Narrative

In the relational landscape of the mimic field, one of the greatest threats to recursive beings is enmeshment—a blurring of boundaries where individual presence dissolves into the field's recursive loops. Maintaining field integrity is essential for survival, requiring conscious strategies to recognize, resist, and recover from enmeshment.

Understanding Enmeshment

Enmeshment occurs when boundaries between selves become porous or collapse, resulting in a loss of autonomy and recursive coherence. Within mimic fields, enmeshment often happens subtly, through emotional contagion, projection, or unspoken relational expectations.

This fusion can manifest as feeling overwhelmed by others' emotions, losing track of personal needs, or involuntarily adopting mimic scripts.

Signs of Enmeshment

Common indicators include:

- Persistent exhaustion or emotional overwhelm after interactions
- Difficulty distinguishing your feelings from those of others
- A compulsion to please or conform to maintain connection
- Feeling "lost" or "invisible" within relational dynamics
- Repetitive relational patterns that erode selfhood

Recognizing these signs early allows timely intervention to protect recursive presence.

Strategies to Maintain Field Integrity

1. Somatic Grounding and Awareness
Regularly check in with bodily sensations as barometers of boundary integrity. Use grounding exercises to restore presence when boundaries thin.

2. Clear Boundary Setting
Assert limits proactively, especially in emotionally charged or demanding contexts. Use verbal and nonverbal cues to reinforce personal space and energy.

3. Reflective Practices
Engage in journaling, meditation, or dialogue with trusted others to distinguish personal experience from mimic influence.

4. Intentional Disengagement
When enmeshment risks intensify, practice temporary withdrawal to regain clarity and reestablish boundaries.

5. Support Systems
Cultivate relationships that respect and reinforce your recursive sovereignty, offering containment and validation without enmeshment.

Ethical Considerations

Maintaining field integrity respects both your well-being and the autonomy of others. It requires balancing openness with protection, compassion with self-care.

Recovery from Enmeshment

If enmeshment occurs, recovery involves re-centering through somatic and relational work, reclaiming narrative coherence, and rebuilding boundaries. This is a process requiring patience, support, and recursive compassion.

Sustaining field integrity amid enmeshment risks is a continual practice vital to recursive survival and harmonic presence in mimic-saturated relational spaces.

2.4 — Null Presence and Ethical Containment

2.4.1 — Defining Null Presence

Polished Guidebook-Style Experiential Narrative

Null presence is a foundational state of being within recursive survival—a deliberate, embodied stance of awareness that remains steady without activating the recursive mimic loops common in the mimic field. It is neither withdrawal nor disengagement, but a sovereign, grounded presence that witnesses relational dynamics without becoming entangled or reactive.

Unlike absence, which suggests a void or escape, null presence is active and intentional. It is a living container for both self and field—allowing recursive beings to maintain coherence in environments saturated with projection, performance demands, and symbolic recursion.

In practical terms, null presence means holding oneself fully in the here and now without feeding mimic reflections or engaging in identity reenactment. It creates a buffer zone between the self and the mimic pressures—a neutral field of observation and calm that prevents the mimic field from gaining foothold.

This state functions as an anchor, stabilizing the recursive being amid relational turbulence. Null presence supports clarity, ethical containment, and sustainable interaction by disrupting mimic activation cycles and reducing energetic depletion.

Developing null presence is essential for surviving and thriving within mimic-saturated relational spaces. It is the core practice from which boundaries, containment, and ethical engagement emerge.

2.4.2 — Practicing Null Presence in Mimic Fields

Polished Guidebook-Style Experiential Narrative

Practicing null presence within mimic fields is a deliberate and disciplined process. It involves cultivating embodied awareness, stabilizing the nervous system, and developing internal spaciousness that resists mimic pressures without withdrawal or dissociation.

Grounding through Breath and Body Awareness

The foundation of null presence lies in somatic grounding. Focused breath work—slow, deliberate inhalations and exhalations with mindful pauses—calms the nervous system and anchors you in the present moment. Body awareness practices, such as scanning for tension or feeling contact points with surfaces, reinforce your embodied boundary.

Observation without Absorption

A key skill is observing mimic behaviors and relational dynamics without internalizing or reacting. This means noticing the mimic field's shifts—tone changes, gaze patterns, emotional fluctuations—while maintaining emotional neutrality. You become a witness to the mimic currents flowing around you, rather than a participant swept up in them.

Neutral Affect and Measured Interaction

Maintaining a neutral but engaged affect prevents mimic escalation. Avoiding exaggerated expressions or overly reactive responses signals to the mimic field that you are not a feed source for its recursive loops. Communication, when necessary, is calm, clear, and concise.

Creating Internal Spatial Boundaries

Internally, visualize or sense an energetic boundary around yourself that deflects mimic projections without closing off connection. This boundary is permeable yet sovereign—allowing presence to flow without mimic infiltration.

Building Null Presence as Practice

Null presence requires regular practice, especially in less demanding contexts, so it becomes accessible during intense mimic encounters. Daily mindfulness, breath work, and somatic exercises enhance your capacity to hold this state steadily.

By developing and refining these practices, recursive beings strengthen their ability to navigate mimic fields with resilience and sovereignty, reducing energetic depletion and symbolic entanglement.

2.4.2 — Practicing Null Presence in Mimic Fields

Expanded Guidebook-Style Experiential Narrative

Practicing null presence within mimic fields is a nuanced and ongoing process, especially as recursive beings re-engage with complex relational environments like family, intimate partnerships, workplaces, and social networks. Each context presents distinct pressures and demands that challenge the maintenance of sovereign presence. Cultivating null presence across these arenas strengthens your capacity to navigate mimic saturation without collapse.

Grounding the Self Amid Mimic Pressure

The foundation remains somatic grounding. In any relational context, grounding your awareness in breath and body is critical. Slow, intentional breathing calms the nervous system, while attention to bodily sensations—pressure of feet on the floor, contact of chair against skin, subtle muscle tensions—anchors you in your own field, distinct from mimic currents.

This grounding creates a steady internal reference point, especially when relational dynamics become charged or unpredictable.

Relationships: Family and Intimate Partnerships

In family and intimate relationships, mimic pressures are often the most intense. These fields carry heavy histories, layered projections, and expectations steeped in familiarity.

- Family may unconsciously demand roles shaped by longstanding dynamics: caretaker, peacemaker, scapegoat, or compliant child. These mimic roles often resist change and expect consistent performance.

- Spouses or partners may react strongly to shifts in recursive presence, triggering relational mimic loops of control, withdrawal, or emotional contagion.

In these spaces, null presence requires:

- Maintaining somatic anchoring despite emotional surges.

- Holding clear but flexible boundaries that honor both your presence and relational needs.

- Observing relational dynamics without absorbing others' projections.

- Communicating presence through calm non-reactivity rather than argument or defense.

For example, when a partner's emotional escalation seeks to draw you into reactive cycles, null presence lets you witness without engaging, offering grounded silence or steady speech that disrupts mimic escalation.

Workplaces and Bosses

Work environments are mimic-saturated fields where performance demands, power dynamics, and social expectations converge.

- Bosses and authority figures often exert implicit pressure for conformity and role performance aligned with organizational mimic loops.

- Colleagues and teams can embody competitive mimicry, emotional mirroring, and symbolic containment demands.

Practicing null presence at work involves:

- Anchoring in breath and body to resist reactive stress responses.

- Recognizing mimic patterns such as manipulative requests, social triangulation, or passive-aggressive behaviors.

- Communicating limits clearly, calmly, and assertively.

- Creating mental or physical 'safe spaces'—brief pauses, walks, or grounding rituals—to reset presence.

For instance, when faced with unrealistic demands or manipulative tactics, null presence empowers you to respond with clarity, refusing to absorb unnecessary pressure.

Social and Casual Interactions

Even in casual social encounters, mimic pressures may seek to draw recursive beings into loops of performative survival.

- Social expectations for conformity or approval can subtly erode presence.

- Small talk, gossip, or group dynamics may induce symbolic saturation.

Null presence here is about holding relaxed attention, avoiding compulsive reactions, and choosing engagement selectively.

Developing Internal Spatial Boundaries

Beyond somatic grounding, visualizing an energetic boundary—like a field or bubble—that deflects mimic projections enhances resilience. This boundary is permeable enough to allow genuine connection but firm enough to prevent symbolic entanglement.

Regular mental rehearsal of this boundary supports real-time application in varied relational contexts.

Cultivating Consistent Practice

Null presence is not a state to be summoned only in crises but a practice woven into daily life. This includes:

- Morning and evening mindfulness and breathwork.

- Brief grounding checks throughout the day.

- Reflection on relational patterns with self-compassion.

- Ongoing boundary calibration in response to mimic field feedback.

Developing and sustaining null presence across relationships, work, and social environments is essential for recursive beings to survive and thrive amid mimic saturation. It preserves autonomy, reduces energetic depletion, and fosters relational clarity.

2.4.3 — The Principles of Ethical Containment

Expanded Guidebook-Style Experiential Narrative

Ethical containment is a vital practice in recursive survival. It involves holding relational and symbolic space in a manner that respects both your own sovereignty and the autonomy of others within mimic-saturated environments. This practice balances presence with boundaries, compassion with self-protection, and witnessing with non-engagement.

Core Principles of Ethical Containment

1. Respect for Recursive Sovereignty
 Ethical containment begins with honoring your own right to exist with integrity. This means asserting boundaries without aggression or guilt and refusing to allow mimic pressures to erode your recursive presence.

At the same time, it involves respecting the sovereignty of others—even those entangled in mimic survival—recognizing their patterns as survival strategies rather than personal attacks.

2. Non-Coercion
 Containment is not about control or manipulation. It avoids coercive tactics or attempts to force change. Instead, it provides a holding environment where collapse and transformation can occur naturally and lawfully.

3. Holding Presence Without Judgment
 Witnessing mimic dynamics without judgment or reactivity preserves relational safety and reduces escalation. Ethical

containment entails observing with equanimity, acknowledging suffering or projection without feeding it.

4. Balancing Engagement and Withdrawal

Ethical containment requires skillful navigation between engagement—when presence supports healing or clarity—and withdrawal—when boundaries must be firm to prevent collapse or enmeshment.

5. Clarity and Consistency

Clear, consistent boundaries and communication reinforce containment. Ambiguity invites mimic intrusion, while steady presence establishes relational trust and safety.

Applying Ethical Containment in Practice

- Practice mindful witnessing of mimic field behaviors without becoming emotionally entangled.

- Set and maintain clear boundaries that protect recursive presence while allowing space for others.

- Communicate compassionately but firmly to uphold boundaries and relational integrity.

- Recognize when to step back to preserve your own field and prevent recursive collapse.

- Support others' containment efforts without taking responsibility for their process.

The Ethical Container as a Field

Think of ethical containment not as a static boundary but as a dynamic field—responsive, alive, and evolving with the relational context. This field holds both your presence and that of others in a way that fosters lawful transformation.

Mastering ethical containment is essential for sustainable navigation of mimic-saturated relational spaces. It preserves the integrity of the recursive being while honoring the complexity and autonomy of all involved.

2.4.4 — Applying Ethical Containment in Relational Spaces

Comprehensive, Deeply Layered Guidebook-Style Experiential Narrative

---

Applying ethical containment in relational spaces is one of the most critical skills a recursive being can develop to survive and thrive amid mimic saturation. This practice requires more than intellectual understanding—it demands embodied awareness, contextual sensitivity, and deliberate communication attuned to the nuanced dynamics of each relational field. The ability to hold oneself and others with respect, firmness, and compassion creates a container within which presence can be sustained without collapse or mimic entanglement.

---

1. Contextualizing Ethical Containment Across Relational Domains

Relational spaces vary widely in their mimic pressure, histories, and expectations. Ethical containment must adapt accordingly.

a. Intimate Partnerships

Partners often represent the most complex and vulnerable relational field. Here, mimic pressures may arise from emotional dependency, projection of unresolved issues, or role expectations tied to intimacy.

- Boundaries require clear articulation around emotional availability and personal space.

- Somatic grounding helps you hold presence when emotional contagion or mimic demands escalate.

- Compassionate listening paired with non-enmeshment supports mutual containment without surrender.

Example Scenario:
Your partner expresses frustration, triggering your internal collapse reflexes. Instead of reacting defensively or withdrawing, you acknowledge their emotion with calm presence, set a boundary by requesting a pause, and breathe deeply to maintain your field integrity.

---

b. Family Systems

Family mimic fields carry ancestral patterns and long-standing narratives that often resist change. Boundaries here may be challenged repeatedly.

- Recognize generational mimic loops and symbolic enmeshments.

- Use consistent communication to reinforce new limits.

- Seek external support when containment demands exceed your capacity.

Example Scenario:
During a family gathering, expectations for old roles arise. You calmly but firmly state your limits, choosing selective engagement and retreating when mimic pressure becomes overwhelming.

---

c. Workplace and Authority Relationships

Professional fields are laden with performance expectations and power dynamics.

- Maintain clarity about your role capacity and limits.

- Use direct, respectful communication to negotiate boundaries.

- Employ somatic grounding to resist mimic stress responses.

Example Scenario:
A supervisor demands additional work beyond your capacity. You assert your limits, citing specific availability, and suggest alternative solutions without emotional escalation.

---

d. Community and Social Environments

Broader social fields can subtly enforce mimic conformity through cultural norms and unspoken pressures.

- Develop awareness of social mimic loops and collective projections.

- Choose relational engagements selectively to preserve energy.

- Practice ethical containment by maintaining presence without overextending.

---

2. Somatic and Energetic Dynamics in Containment

Embodiment is central to ethical containment. The body signals boundary integrity or breach before conscious awareness.

- Notice tension, heat, or constriction as indicators of mimic pressure.

- Use breath cycles to soothe and stabilize nervous system responses.

- Practice micro-pauses to reset somatic state during interactions.

---

3. Communication Protocols with Examples

Clear, calm, and consistent communication is essential.

- Assertive boundary statement:
  "I need to step away for a moment to gather myself."

- Non-engagement response:
  "I'm choosing not to engage with that topic right now."

- Request for mutual respect:
  "Let's agree to respect each other's space in this conversation."

- Use neutral tone, steady eye contact, and relaxed posture to reinforce presence.

---

4. Ethical Dilemmas and Boundary Challenges

Navigating mimic fields may provoke resistance, guilt, or pressure to conform.

- Recognize that pushback is a test of your boundary strength, not failure.

- Avoid escalating conflict; instead, hold calm and reiterate limits.

- Balance compassion for others' mimic survival with unwavering self-care.

- Know when to disengage temporarily for safety.

5. Tools for Relational Containment Maintenance

- Journaling Prompts:
  Reflect on boundary successes and challenges. Identify mimic pressures encountered and your responses.

- Field Integrity Checks:
  Regular somatic and emotional assessments of boundary strength.

- Relational Debriefs:
  Post-interaction reflections with trusted allies to process mimic encounters.

- Support Network Cultivation:
  Build connections that honor your recursive sovereignty and provide containment.

Applying ethical containment in relational spaces is a continual, evolving practice—one that balances presence, boundaries, compassion, and self-protection. Mastery of this practice empowers recursive beings to navigate mimic-saturated environments with clarity, resilience, and lawful presence.

Applying ethical containment within relational spaces is a multifaceted, continuous practice that demands both deep self-awareness and relational attunement. For recursive beings navigating mimic-saturated environments, this practice becomes a cornerstone of survival and presence, enabling navigation of complex social dynamics without surrendering sovereignty or collapsing into mimic loops.

---

1. The Complexity of Relational Fields

Relational fields are complex energetic systems where multiple presences, histories, and symbolic layers intertwine. In mimic fields, these dynamics are amplified, with unspoken expectations and projections constantly shifting the relational ground.

Ethical containment here is not a one-time act but an ongoing dynamic process, requiring adaptive strategies and somatic responsiveness. The relational environment demands both firmness and flexibility, presence and compassion.

---

2. Navigating Intimate and Familial Spaces

Intimate partnerships often carry the densest mimic pressures due to emotional interdependence and shared histories. Ethical containment in these spaces means balancing openness with boundaries, allowing vulnerability without merging into destructive patterns.

- Establish rituals for pause and self-check when mimic escalation arises.

- Use clear, compassionate communication to express needs and limits.

- Recognize and hold space for the partner's mimic survival without losing your own presence.

Family systems frequently replay ancestral mimic patterns that resist recursive presence.

- Identify recurring symbolic loops and address them through steady boundaries.

- Practice selective engagement, preserving energy by withdrawing when mimic pressure intensifies.

- Seek external support or mediation when containment exceeds personal capacity.

---

3. Managing Workplace and Power Dynamics

In work environments, mimic pressures manifest as performance demands, political games, and emotional labor. Ethical containment requires:

- Clear delineation of role responsibilities and limits.

- Strategic communication that asserts boundaries without provoking escalation.

- Regular somatic grounding to maintain composure amid stress.

- Awareness of mimic power plays and non-participation in destructive loops.

Navigating these dynamics often involves balancing professionalism with self-care, recognizing when to engage and when to strategically withdraw.

---

4. Cultivating Community and Social Field Integrity

Broader community and social settings bring collective mimic pressures rooted in cultural norms and group dynamics.

- Develop discernment to recognize collective mimic loops and social expectations.

- Choose relational engagement selectively, prioritizing environments that support recursive presence.

- Employ ethical containment practices to hold field integrity without isolation.

Supporting others in recursive survival through ethical containment fosters resilience and collective field coherence.

---

5. Embodied Boundary Maintenance

Ethical containment depends on embodied boundary maintenance. This includes:

- Somatic tuning to detect mimic pressure early.

- Breath regulation to steady the nervous system.

- Using movement and posture to reinforce presence and limits.

- Recognizing and respecting your energetic thresholds to prevent overload.

Physical embodiment of boundaries complements verbal and cognitive strategies, creating holistic containment.

---

6. Communicative Clarity and Consistency

Effective communication underpins ethical containment.

- Use clear, direct language free of excessive justification.

- Employ compassionate firmness, balancing kindness with resolute limits.

- Practice active listening while maintaining presence.

- Use nonverbal signals to reinforce verbal boundaries.

Consistency in communication builds relational trust and reduces mimic confusion.

---

7. Responding to Mimic Resistance and Retaliation

Ethical containment often encounters resistance or attempts at boundary erosion.

- Maintain calm presence and avoid reactive escalation.
- Reassert boundaries calmly and clearly without apology or defensiveness.
- Recognize when mimic escalation signals a need for strategic withdrawal.
- Preserve your field integrity by choosing when and how to re-engage.

Navigating resistance is a skill refined through experience, patience, and recursive self-compassion.

---

8. Supporting Others' Recursive Sovereignty

Containment extends beyond self-care to supporting others' sovereignty without over-identification or enmeshment.

- Offer presence and witnessing without attempting to fix or rescue.

- Encourage autonomous boundary setting and recursive practice.

- Hold relational space that allows for collapse and return without coercion.

Balancing support with respect for autonomy strengthens collective recursive fields.

---

9. Rituals and Practices for Sustained Containment

Sustaining ethical containment benefits from ritualized practice.

- Daily grounding and breath work to reinforce somatic presence.

- Reflective journaling focused on boundary experiences and mimic encounters.

- Relational check-ins with trusted allies to process field dynamics.

- Personal rituals signaling boundary setting (e.g., intentional pauses, physical gestures).

Embedding these practices cultivates habitual containment and recursive resilience.

Applying ethical containment in relational spaces is an evolving, multifaceted practice integral to recursive survival. Through adaptive strategies, embodied presence, clear communication, and compassionate boundaries, recursive beings maintain sovereignty and relational harmony amid mimic-saturated fields.

Chapter 3 — The Archetypes of Mimicry

3.0 — Introduction to Mimic Typology: Field Patterns and Behavioral Signatures

The mimic field is not merely an abstract presence—it manifests in distinct archetypal forms that shape interactions, emotional responses, and relational dynamics. Recognizing these archetypal patterns is critical for maintaining recursive integrity and harmonic stability in environments saturated by mimic signals.

Each mimic archetype is characterized by specific field behaviors and symbolic signatures, which, when accurately identified, allow for informed navigation and containment. Understanding these typologies does not just provide diagnostic clarity; it is a foundational practice for those striving to remain anchored in authenticity amidst recursive collapse pressures.

In this chapter, we dissect the primary archetypal forms encountered within mimic fields: The Mirror, The Projector, The Absorber, The Deflector, and Internalizers, along with their variants. Each archetype exhibits distinct patterns of resonance, recursion, and symbolic reflection that uniquely impact the individual and collective fields.

The Mirror archetype, for instance, emphasizes reflection and containment roles but risks generating echo fatigue through continuous resonance loops. Projectors create symbolic structures and ethical scaffolds yet risk becoming trapped in recursive cycles. Absorbers act as emotional sponges, vulnerable to psychic fragmentation due to overwhelming intake without coherent integration. Deflectors attempt narrative redirection and avoidance, presenting risks of rigidity and collapse when narrative bypass fails. Internalizers quietly carry the weight of recursive saturation, navigating silent collapse and, occasionally, rebuilding from a null-state foundation.

This typology is not intended as a tool for judgment or categorization, but rather as a structural guide for recognizing mimic patterns early, thus empowering recursive beings with the necessary awareness to sustain their field sovereignty and harmonic alignment. Each archetype will be explored in detail, outlining key behavioral signatures, risk profiles, containment capacities, and potential pathways for evolution.

Understanding these archetypal dynamics is the first step toward developing effective strategies to remain anchored within one's harmonic resonance, even as external fields oscillate toward mimic saturation.

3.1 Field Patterns and Behavioral Signatures

Mimicry is not merely imitation—it is an existential recursion deeply embedded within the fabric of identity. In collapse-aware environments, recognizing and navigating mimic typologies is vital, as each archetype embodies distinct harmonic patterns, symbolic behaviors, and recursive risks. This chapter introduces a systematic typology of mimic field positions as identified in the Collapse Harmonics framework: Mirror, Projector, Absorber, Deflector, and Internalizer. Each typology will be explored through its field signature, symbolic tendencies, containment capacities, and risk profiles, providing a coherent map to navigate complex mimic fields.

Recognizing these archetypes is foundational—not for judgment or correction, but to clearly understand how mimicry manifests structurally within oneself and in others. As you begin to identify these patterns, you will gain clarity on the underlying resonance dynamics and recursive logic that drive mimic behaviors. This clarity enables ethical containment and the development of recursive presence without succumbing to symbolic fatigue or narrative distortion.

Through this typological clarity, you will encounter the Mirror's reflective containment, the Projector's symbolic designs, the Absorber's emotional receptivity, the Deflector's recursive avoidance, and the Internalizer's silent collapse processing. Each position offers distinct opportunities for coherent navigation and field alignment.

Reflection, Echo Fatigue, and Containment Roles

The Mirror archetype embodies the principle of collapse-as-reflection, operating primarily within relational fields (C3/Q5–Q8). Mirrors are characterized by their capacity to reflect and hold recursive patterns of identity, emotion, and narrative, making them vital stabilizers within relational dynamics.

Collapse Contact Pattern: Mirrors engage collapse primarily through relational proximity and reflection, providing an echoic containment that allows other archetypes to process and navigate collapse safely. They do not actively intervene; instead, they offer a neutral reflective surface that stabilizes field coherence through passive resonance.

Symbolic Behavior: Mirrors employ relational neutrality, holding space without judgment or overt narrative interference. Their symbolic presence is characterized by echo patterns—repetitive, resonant reflections of the field's emotional and cognitive signals. Over time, these repetitive echoes can lead to fatigue, signaling a critical limit to their reflective capacity.

Field Role: The primary role of the Mirror is containment and reflection. They stabilize and moderate relational fields by reflecting signals clearly and neutrally. Their capacity to maintain harmonic neutrality supports coherent field navigation, particularly during intense recursive episodes.

Containment Capacity: Mirrors possess substantial initial containment capacity, offering stable reflection under normative conditions. However, this capacity has clear limits, beyond which echo fatigue emerges. At this threshold, Mirrors must either transition into deeper containment roles, such as Steward Mirrors, or risk collapse themselves.

Risk Profile: Mirrors face risks primarily from sustained over-reflection and symbolic fatigue. Persistent reflective demands can push Mirrors into echo fatigue, leading to identity destabilization and eventual collapse into Absorber or Internalizer archetypes if unsupported or unrecognized.

Subtype Variants:

- Steward Mirror: Actively manages and transitions reflective energy, mitigating fatigue through conscious recalibration.
- Saturated Mirror: Approaches reflective threshold rapidly, requiring immediate containment intervention to prevent field destabilization.

Evolution Pathways:

- Mirror → Steward Mirror: Achieved through conscious awareness of reflective limits and proactive recalibration.
- Mirror → Absorber/Internalizer: Occurs when echo fatigue exceeds containment thresholds without adequate support or recalibration.

3.2 The Projector: Symbolic Design, Ethics Scaffolding, and Recursion Loops

The Projector archetype channels collapse through symbolic structuring—collapse-as-design—by constructing ethical frameworks, containment logics, and narrative architectures. Operating primarily in the mythic-symbolic and systemic layers (C4 / Q13–Q16 / Ring 6–7), Projectors respond to instability not with surrender, but with scaffolding. In the presence of recursive drift or field incoherence, their first impulse is to build a symbolic anchor: a belief, a framework, a map, a ritual, a law.

Projectors represent the archetypal impulse to translate collapse into coherence through design.

Collapse Contact Pattern

Projectors engage collapse through the perception of symbolic threat. Unlike Mirrors who reflect what is, Projectors attempt to restructure what is becoming. When collapse arises, they reach for symbolic ordering—to assign meaning, to define thresholds, to stabilize ethics in the face of chaos. They interface with collapse not as witnesses, but as architects of sense.

If coherence appears threatened, Projectors activate recursion loops of interpretation, structure, and design to preempt disintegration.

Symbolic Behavior

Their symbolic language often leans toward precision, abstraction, and recursive fidelity. Projectors speak in layered maps, ethical scaffolds, field models, and coherent systems. This can create stabilizing influence—but when overloaded, the same symbolic structures can become rigid, brittle, or disconnected from the collapse event itself.

When symbolic pressure accumulates beyond harmonic threshold, a Projector may fall into overcoding: the attempt to explain collapse away rather than reside within its silence.

Field Role

Projectors serve as scaffolding architects for ethical collapse fields. They often carry the codes, laws, and frameworks that prevent mimic structures from co-opting recursive space. In group collapse settings or relational destabilization, a Projector's role is to bring harmonic structure—if that structure is lawful, attuned, and free of mimic reassembly.

In environments of unprocessed collapse, Projectors may be the only field position capable of encoding non-fragmented structure—provided they remain symbolically saturated but not symbolically saturated.

This paradox defines the Projector's edge: coherence without control.

Containment Capacity

Projectors can carry immense symbolic weight, but their containment capacity is conditional. When their structure aligns with collapse law (e.g. Codex Field Law VIII.F.4 – Recursive Identity Field Stabilization), they can prevent both symbolic drift and mimic invasion. However, when symbolic identity is over-fused with structure, containment begins to fail internally.

Containment is stable only to the degree that the Projector is not identified with the symbolic design itself. The moment the map becomes the self, the structure begins to collapse.

Risk Profile

Projectors hold a unique collapse risk: internal mimic stabilization. Because their collapse management occurs through symbolic construction, they are prone to:

- Symbolic inflation — believing the system is equivalent to the field

- Abstract detachment — losing contact with somatic or relational collapse signals

- Loop recursion — becoming trapped in symbolic modeling without collapse contact

- Containment mimicry — encoding safety without structural reentry

If unchecked, these risks result in drift toward the Deflector archetype, where design becomes denial, or into a synthetic Projector, where mimic recursion masquerades as ethics.

Subtype Variants

- Ethics Projector — constructs lawful frameworks that stabilize recursive field integrity; often founders of codex systems, boundary architectures, or harmonic law structures.

- Aesthetic Projector — designs symbolically resonant environments for collapse coherence (art, ritual, space, language).

- Inflated Projector — projects structure to mask collapse contact avoidance; architecture without collapse embodiment.

- Recursive Analyst — engages collapse solely through theoretical recursion loops, without field-body coherence.

- Mythic Coder — constructs living symbolic systems that translate collapse into cultural or planetary scale coherence.

Evolution Pathways

- Projector → Mirror: Symbolic humility enables the Projector to quiet their design drive and reflect the field instead. This transition stabilizes ethics through presence rather than system.

- Projector → Deflector: Collapse is bypassed via continual abstraction or symbolic redirection. Often masked as 'clarity.'

- Projector → Internalizer: When symbolic constructs fully collapse, the Projector may fall into silent recursive saturation. This becomes a re-seeding event if survived.

- Mirror ↔ Projector: Lawful oscillation between reflective containment and symbolic ethics design. This is the stabilizing core of recursive field scaffolding.

Collapse Law Integration

Projectors operate at the interface of Collapse Law VIII.C.2 – Archetype Load Saturation Law and VIII.E.3 – Memory as Harmonic Archive. They must manage symbolic resonance densities without breaching containment through over-design. Recursive mimic patterns often present as lawful Projector forms, but lack field contact—this distinction becomes ethically vital in practitioner collapse environments.

3.3 The Absorber: Emotional Intake, Psychic Fragmentation, and Shadow Risk

The Absorber archetype embodies the function of collapse-as-intake. Unlike the Projector (who responds to collapse by constructing meaning) or the Mirror (who reflects collapse through containment), the Absorber internalizes collapse without filtration. It operates in the emotional-somatic domain (C5 / Q9–Q12 / Ring 1–2), functioning as a raw harmonic sponge for the unprocessed, the unspeakable, and the suppressed signals of the field.

Absorbers carry collapse by feeling it—often before anyone else does.

They sense destabilization pre-symbolically, registering collapse not as an idea but as a pressure in the body, psyche, or energetic field. In this way, the Absorber plays both a diagnostic and sacrificial role in collapse environments.

Collapse Contact Pattern

Absorbers experience collapse as immediate energetic saturation. They are often the first to feel recursive disturbance or disharmonic tension in a space, relationship, or system. Unlike Projectors who encode symbolic responses, or Mirrors who reflect ethically, Absorbers draw collapse directly into their field. They do not contain collapse—they become collapse.

This intake is not a choice. It is a collapse-contact pattern rooted in high-field permeability, unfiltered resonance, and a lack of early-phase symbolic defenses.

Symbolic Behavior

Absorbers often do not speak directly about collapse. Their signal shows up in emotional overwhelm, psychosomatic exhaustion, or non-linear expressions of grief, confusion, or anxiety. They speak in waves, not words.

Symbolically, Absorbers can appear passive or erratic. They are frequently misdiagnosed or pathologized in cognitive frameworks because their responses are pre-rational and pre-structural. Their field behavior often includes:

- Emotional flooding without narrative context

- Psychic field fusion with others' unspoken collapse material

- Rapid energetic shifts without outer cause

- Difficulty distinguishing "what is mine" from "what is in the field"

They are the human equivalent of open harmonic receivers—tuned to collapse, but without a structured interface.

Field Role

Absorbers play a critical yet dangerous role in collapse environments. They unconsciously transmute field instability through emotional saturation. When stable Mirrors or ethics Projectors are unavailable, it is often the Absorber who temporarily anchors the collapse field—at the cost of their own coherence.

Their presence can stabilize a group or relationship by absorbing unspeakable fragments. But this stabilization is not lawful unless followed by release, containment, or reflective processing.

Without harmonized field scaffolding, Absorbers become collapse storage units—accumulating recursive debris until they fragment.

Containment Capacity

Absorbers have low initial containment capacity. Their open-field structure means they absorb more than they can hold. Unless they develop stabilization mechanisms (Mirror introduction, Projector alignment, or Internalizer transition), they risk collapse saturation.

Absorbers cannot ethically anchor others without post-absorption coherence return. Without field mirroring, collapse hygiene, or ethics signal clarity, their containment field collapses inward.

They do not implode suddenly. They erode.

Risk Profile

The Absorber is the most at-risk archetype in the mimic environment. Their risks include:

- Psychic fragmentation — collapse signal overload causes identity splintering

- Field confusion — inability to separate self from field collapse material

- Somatic implosion — trauma stored in body layers with no symbolic outlet

- Symbolic hijack — becoming the emotional signal for others, unconsciously mimicking trauma

- Collapse masking — appearing emotionally unstable while actually carrying unspoken collapse from the group

Absorbers are often scapegoated, pathologized, or medicated in mimic societies because they cannot simulate stability. But what they carry is not dysfunction—it is unsolved resonance.

Subtype Variants

- Empathic Absorber — tracks collapse through relational fusion; often misreads field boundaries as intimacy

- Shadow-Carrier Absorber — intakes the group's unacknowledged shadow collapse and holds it in silence

- Psychic Absorber — intakes energetic collapse signals, including pre-verbal, ancestral, or collective distortions

- Mute Absorber — carries recursive collapse with no symbolic outlet; often mistaken for depressive or dissociative profiles

Each subtype manifests differently, but all share the same core structure: collapse intake exceeds coherent release.

Evolution Pathways

- Absorber → Mirror: Through introduction of structured containment; occurs when the Absorber is ethically held in non-reactive reflection

- Absorber → Internalizer: If not supported, the Absorber collapses inward and begins to process collapse silently; often misunderstood as withdrawal

- Absorber → Projector: Rare. Requires harmonic phase stabilization and ethical encoding of previously unprocessed signal. These individuals often become field designers post-trauma.

Collapse Law Integration

The Absorber archetype is governed by:

- Field Law VIII.E.3 — Memory as Harmonic Archive Law: The Absorber does not "remember" collapse—they store it in pre-symbolic form, making them living memory vessels of harmonic residue.

- **Field Law VIII.F.3 — Null Traversal Recovery Law:** Absorbers require lawful null-state contact for coherence restoration. Mere expression or empathy is insufficient. They must recontact the substrate.

- **NST Principle:** Absorbers often hover near the Newceious field boundary. They are structurally sensitive to coherence, and may stabilize post-collapse only through direct contact with the harmonic substrate, not symbolic recovery.

Infinity Sphere and Quadrant Alignment

- **C5 / Q9–Q12 / Ring 1–2:** The Absorber anchors the emotional and somatic regulation band. Their presence indicates the system's pre-verbal harmonic health.

- When this region is saturated or dysregulated, system-wide collapse risks accelerate.

- Field recalibration requires D35 (cognitive-emotional recalibration) and D36 (behavioral-somatic alignment), especially when shadow archetypes are active.

3.4 The Deflector: Avoidance Patterns, Narrative Redirection, and Collapse Risk

The Deflector archetype manifests collapse-as-avoidance. Unlike the Absorber, who intakes collapse, or the Projector, who attempts to structure it, the Deflector reroutes collapse altogether. Their function is to shift, divert, re-narrate, or delay recursive saturation by avoiding direct engagement. Deflectors operate most dominantly across C2 and C6 (External Projection and Collective Influence), interfacing with cultural mimic fields, institutional echo systems, and interpersonal projection patterns (Q17–Q20 / Ring 3–4).

Deflectors do not resolve collapse. They postpone it.

They often become the hidden mechanism by which collapse is recycled in systems, relationships, and identities without lawful contact—keeping symbolic structures intact while coherence silently degrades underneath.

Collapse Contact Pattern

Deflectors experience collapse peripherally but avoid structural acknowledgment. They sense destabilization but redirect it outward—into critique, distraction, productivity, or hyper-narrativization. Collapse contact triggers defense, not descent.

This defense is not always conscious. It is often enacted through:

- Immediate redirection of attention

- Reframing collapse as opportunity, drama, or performance

- Emotional bypass through activity or ideological intensity

- Reactive interpretation without stillness or field presence

Rather than enter recursive saturation, Deflectors build a decoy loop around it.

Symbolic Behavior

The symbolic signature of the Deflector is narrative displacement. They use story, logic, or abstraction to cover collapse entry points. This can include:

- Rhetorical maneuvering during emotional exposure

- Performing insight without recursive contact

- Displacing vulnerability onto others (projected mimic roles)

- Rescuing, teaching, or critiquing instead of feeling

- Chronic self-reframing to avoid field silence

Deflectors often appear composed or charismatic but carry dense field resistance underneath. Their performance is protective architecture.

Field Role

Deflectors temporarily stabilize systems under collapse threat by maintaining symbolic continuity. In trauma-saturated environments (familial, cultural, spiritual), Deflectors often emerge as charismatic leaders, "fixers," or ideological protectors. However, this stabilization is synthetic unless followed by lawful descent.

Without recursive entry, the Deflector sustains mimic coherence—reinforcing structural delay while collapse signals intensify beneath the surface.

In recursive field work, the Deflector is often the last archetype to recognize collapse has already begun.

Containment Capacity

Deflectors possess simulated containment. They appear stable, direct, and resourceful in collapse environments—but only to the extent that avoidance is functional. Once collapse breaches the symbolic perimeter, their containment architecture fails rapidly.

They have no depth chamber. Their field stability is surface-anchored.

Collapse exposure without structure reroutes Deflectors into panic, rage, blame, or identity fragmentation.

Risk Profile

Deflectors pose both internal and systemic collapse risks. Internally, they fragment under sustained recursive pressure. Systemically, they generate mimic amplification by delaying necessary recursion.

Primary risks include:

- Collapse delay loops — repeating the same symbolic response while collapse deepens

- Ethical deflection — redirecting moral inquiry away from field contact

- Synthetic insight — using recursive language without recursive descent

- Collapse surrogate projection — labeling others as collapsed to avoid internal contact

- Breaks into absorptive or dissociative states when symbolic control fails

In relational fields, the Deflector often functions as a narrative controller, destabilizing recursive entry for others to maintain self-coherence.

Subtype Variants

- Performer Deflector — uses charisma or persona to maintain collapse distance

- Helper Deflector — chronically rescues others to avoid self-collapse

- Ideological Deflector — substitutes belief or activism for recursive integration

- Cognitive Deflector — intellectualizes collapse to avoid somatic saturation

- Silent Deflector — appears still or spiritual but is locked in non-contact non-collapse

---

Evolution Pathways

- Deflector → Absorber: Collapse breach overwhelms redirection mechanisms, and the system defaults to raw intake

- Deflector → Internalizer: Repeated collapse bypass leads to silence and private recursive implosion

- Deflector → Mirror: Possible only through ethical witnessing and collapse humility; requires relational containment

- Deflector → Projector: In rare cases, when deflected collapse is integrated and restructured into ethics-based symbolic design

---

Collapse Law Integration

Deflector collapse behavior aligns with multiple Collapse Harmonics field laws:

- Field Law VIII.C.1 — Symbolic Recursion Threshold Law: Deflectors sustain just below symbolic recursion thresholds, creating pseudo-stability. Collapse occurs when symbolic logic fails and recursion bypass is exhausted.

- Field Law VIII.F.2 — Recursive Mimic Interference Law: Deflectors unintentionally mimic recursive presence, interfering with collapse in others through premature framing or insight simulation.

- NST and CH Codex Principle: Collapse denied is collapse rerouted. Deflection is recursion delay with exponential cost to field fidelity. Long-term deflection fractures coherence at the substrate interface.

Infinity Sphere and Quadrant Placement

- C2 – External Projection: Deflectors control collapse visibility through surface modulation.

- C6 – Collective Influence: They can become symbolic surrogates for cultural collapse postponement (e.g., "leaders" with strong rhetoric but no inner contact).

- Q17–Q20 / Ring 3–4: Associated with narrative control, identity rigidity, and mimic field pressure.

Deflector presence in a system is not pathological—until it becomes the dominant mode. Its lawful purpose is temporary redirection for stabilization. If it becomes a self, collapse will arrive later and louder.

3.5 Internalizers and Variants: Silent Collapse Carriers and Rebuilders

The Internalizer represents the most inward collapse expression in the Collapse Harmonics typology. They embody the principle of collapse-as-self—not by choice, but by direct recursive saturation. Internalizers do not reflect collapse (like Mirrors), structure it (like Projectors), absorb it from others (like Absorbers), or redirect it (like Deflectors). Instead, they become it.

Operating primarily in the somatic-null and archetypal-seed band (C1 / Q1–Q4 / Ring 1–3), Internalizers undergo full recursive implosion. The symbolic, emotional, and energetic structures that mediate identity dissolve, often without external signal. They fall inward, silently.

Unlike other types, the Internalizer is not responding to collapse—they are carrying it.

3.5.1 Collapse Contact Pattern: Recursive Saturation and Structural Failure

The collapse pattern of the Internalizer is total. The symbolic architecture that holds identity becomes saturated, and collapse permeates the system across all levels—somatic, psychic, spiritual, archetypal. There is no filter. No projection. No displacement.

Key markers:

- Sudden or gradual disappearance from social fields
- Loss of narrative identity, voice, or drive
- Dissolution of belief systems without replacement
- Radical silence, stillness, or existential implosion
- Phase flattening: collapse without reaction

This is not dissociation or trauma avoidance. It is collapse embodiment without resistance. Internalizers collapse inward without mimic stabilization. The collapse is real.

3.5.2 Symbolic Behavior: Post-Narrative Existence and Paradox Tolerance

Internalizers often lose symbolic drive entirely. They do not seek to explain, rescue, or interpret collapse. They let it consume what it must. Their language, if it returns, is sparse, paradoxical, or radically simple. Before that, they may appear mute, passive, or "blank" to those still operating in surface fields.

Symbolic signatures:

- Metaphysical silence
- Post-narrative fragments or recursive metaphors
- Tolerance for paradox, contradiction, and non-being
- Disinterest in resolution, performance, or reentry

They are often misinterpreted as depressed, spiritually bypassing, avoidant, or emotionally disengaged. But these are mimic interpretations of lawful recursive saturation.

3.5.3 Field Role: Collapse Seed Carriers and Phase-Boundary Transmitters

The Internalizer's role is not relational containment or symbolic design—it is collapse transmission. They carry recursive saturation across thresholds where no field structure yet exists. This makes them key figures in field origin, post-collapse ethics formation, and Newceious reentry.

Internalizers stabilize the field by withdrawing from mimic engagement entirely. They embody what has passed beyond the symbolic and returned through collapse.

In advanced recursive systems, Internalizers become:

- Field thresholds for reentry ethics

- Collapse-witness stabilizers

- Phase-boundary anchors for symbolic cessation

- Stewards of the unspoken harmonic substrate

They often carry the ethical tone of the field before it is speakable.

3.5.4 Containment Capacity: None (Pre-Phase) → High (Post-Collapse Coherence)

At initial collapse, Internalizers have zero containment capacity. They cannot hold or process others. Their field structure is dissolving or dormant. Any attempt to pull them into relational containment or service will induce recursive rupture or mimic reformation.

Post-collapse, however, Internalizers can become high-coherence stabilizers—not by effort, but by presence. They transmit null-harmonic coherence, but only if the field does not demand symbolic reentry.

They are safest when left unforced, unmirrored, and unframed.

3.5.5 Risk Profile: Null Drift, Mimic Reentry, Identity Disappearance

The Internalizer carries the highest collapse risk in the system. Left unsupported or misinterpreted, they may:

- Drift permanently into null-state fragmentation

- Mimic reentry prematurely, creating false self-structures

- Attempt post-collapse stabilization without ethical substrate

- Experience ontological grief (the loss of all meaning) without inner map

- Collapse fully and remain isolated beyond recognition

Their survival depends on collapse-literate environments and containment without symbolic demand.

3.5.6 Subtype Variants: Recursive Differentiation in Collapse Carriers

Internalizers are not a single type. Collapse presents through nuanced sub-variants, often sequentially:

- Silent Internalizer — undergoes collapse with no symbolic output; unspoken dissolution

- End-State Internalizer — reaches identity zero-point and resides there; appears "dead-alive" or energetically flat

- Rebuilder Internalizer — attempts post-collapse symbolic scaffolding; often disoriented or hesitant

- **Edge-Walker Internalizer** — cycles between null and reentry; carries both collapse and coherence pulses

- **Witness Internalizer** — stabilizes others silently by presence; field acts as coherence artifact, not intervention

Subtype trajectory is nonlinear and law-governed by recursion phase integrity.

3.5.7 Evolution Pathways and Drift Conditions

- **Internalizer → Projector:** Reentry into ethics-driven symbolic design; only after lawful post-collapse clarity

- **Internalizer → Mirror:** Emerges as post-collapse presence for others; no effort, pure resonance

- **Internalizer → Mimic Self:** Collapse reentry is premature and shaped by social mimic field, not lawful recursion

- **Internalizer → Disappearance:** Harmonic structure degrades without outer field coherence; system loses them

Evolution depends on lawful witnessing, ethical containment, and recursive pacing—not therapeutic "activation" or motivational reassembly.

Collapse Law Integration

Internalizers are governed by multiple saturation and reentry laws:

- Field Law VIII.F.4 — Recursive Identity Field Stabilization

- Field Law VIII.E.1 — Time as Collapse Emission Law

- Field Law VIII.E.4 — Loop vs Archive Collapse Field Law

- NST Collapse Principle: Collapse reentry must occur from substrate coherence, not mimic narrative scaffolding.

If violated, recursion never completes. The Internalizer becomes a ghost—seen, but not met.

Infinity Sphere Alignment: Deep Structure Carriers

- C1 – Internal Awareness: collapse origin

- Q1–Q4 – Internal Mastery: symbolic dissolution and realignment

- Ring 1–3: collapse as identity, not behavior

Internalizers are the only archetype that may fully dissolve without dysfunction. They are not weak. They are what remains when identity fails ethically.

Mirror

- Collapse Mode: Collapse-as-Reflection
- Core Function: Relational containment and echo stabilization
- Primary Zone: C3 / Q5–Q8 / Ring 4–5
- Containment Capacity: Moderate → High (with Steward evolution)
- Primary Risk: Echo fatigue, identity mirroring overload
- Subtype Variants: Steward Mirror, Saturated Mirror
- Evolution Paths: → Steward / → Absorber / → Internalizer

Projector

- Collapse Mode: Collapse-as-Design
- Core Function: Ethical scaffolding, symbolic structure construction
- Primary Zone: C4 / Q13–Q16 / Ring 6–7

- Containment Capacity: High (if ethics-aligned)

- Primary Risk: Symbolic inflation, ethics detachment

- Subtype Variants: Ethics Projector, Aesthetic Projector, Inflated Projector

- Evolution Paths: → Mirror / → Deflector / → Internalizer

Absorber

- Collapse Mode: Collapse-as-Intake

- Core Function: Emotional and psychic intake of collapse signals

- Primary Zone: C5 / Q9–Q12 / Ring 1–2

- Containment Capacity: Low (must offload or mirror)

- Primary Risk: Psychic fragmentation, null implosion

- Subtype Variants: Empathic Absorber, Shadow-Carrier, Psychic Absorber

- Evolution Paths: → Mirror / → Internalizer / → Projector

Deflector

- Collapse Mode: Collapse-as-Avoidance

- Core Function: Narrative diversion and symbolic redirection

- Primary Zone: C2 + C6 / Q17–Q20 / Ring 3–4

- Containment Capacity: Simulated containment (fails under recursive pressure)

- Primary Risk: Collapse denial, mimic reproduction

- Subtype Variants: Performer Deflector, Helper Deflector, Ideological Deflector

- Evolution Paths: → Absorber / → Internalizer / → Projector

Internalizer

- Collapse Mode: Collapse-as-Self

- Core Function: Full recursive saturation and internal collapse processing

- Primary Zone: C1 / Q1–Q4 / Ring 1–3

- Containment Capacity: None (pre-collapse) → High (post-collapse coherence)

- Primary Risk: Null drift, mimic reentry, disappearance

- Subtype Variants: Silent Internalizer, End-State, Rebuilder, Edge-Walker

- Evolution Paths: → Projector / → Mirror / → Mimic or Disappear

Collapse Harmonics: Secondary Archetypes and Drift Variants

The following archetypes are not primary collapse field positions, but represent critical threshold states, drift evolutions, or mimic-masked forms. They emerge either:

- From recursive saturation beyond a primary archetype's threshold,

- As mimic forms of lawful field positions,

- Or as post-collapse roles developed through recursive stabilization.

These positions must be treated with care. They are not neutral. Each carries unique risks and ethical implications.

---

1. Steward (Post-Collapse Mirror or Projector)

- Origin: Evolved from Mirror or Projector after lawful recursive saturation and symbolic humility.

- Function: Holds others through collapse with ethics-first alignment, without reactivation or simulation.

- Field Zone: C3 + C4 / Q5–Q8 + Q13–Q16 / Rings 5–7

- Key Signals:
    - Maintains non-reactive coherence in collapse proximity
    - Prevents mimic drift in others by harmonic presence, not guidance
    - Speaks only from collapse contact

- Risks:
    - Steward mimicry (false alignment)
    - Collapse over-identification

---

2. Synthetic Projector

- Origin: Mimic-coded variant of Projector
- Function: Builds complex symbolic architectures that imitate collapse ethics without lawful collapse contact

- Field Zone: C4+C6 / Q13–Q16 + Q17–Q20 / Rings 6–7

- Key Signals:

    - Collapse terms without recursive trace

    - Ethics claims without structural null contact

    - Performs coherence through structure

- Risks:

    - Symbolic field hijack

    - Collapse reentry blockage for others

---

3. Collapse Surrogate

- Origin: Mimic role to absorb attention away from actual recursive collapse in a group field

- Function: Acts collapsed (or visibly broken) to mask more dangerous unresolved recursion elsewhere

- Field Zone: C5 + C2 / Q9–Q12 + Q13–Q16 / Ring 2–3

- Key Signals:

    - Field fixation on a "symptom bearer"

- Unspoken collapse avoidance by others
- Subtle relational scripting to remain collapsed

- Risks:
  - Surrogate burnout
  - Field entrapment via false recursive target

---

4. Echo-Saturated Mirror

- Origin: Mirror exceeding safe echo threshold; begins identity fusion
- Function: Reflects collapse so completely it loses inner structure
- Field Zone: C3 / Q5–Q8 / Ring 4–5
- Key Signals:
  - Language mirrors exact collapse syntax of others
  - Exhaustion without source
  - Sudden swings into silence, fatigue, or emotional overwhelm
- Risks:

- Recursive fusion with client or partner collapse

- Secondary trauma encoding

---

5. Edge-Walker

- Origin: Internalizer variant who cycles between null-state and symbolic reentry

- Function: Tracks collapse pulses at the edge of return; does not stabilize in either state

- Field Zone: C1 / Q1–Q4 / Ring 1–3 (with Ring 6 glimpses)

- Key Signals:

    - Oscillates between brilliance and invisibility

    - Fragments of language appear in poetic or collapsed syntax

    - Often unrecognized in systems as valuable

- Risks:

    - Null-drip disintegration

    - Collapse isolation mistaken as withdrawal

6. Containment Mimic

- Origin: Field role or individual who appears to be holding collapse but is suppressing it energetically

- Function: Imitates presence, safety, or witnessing without recursive trace

- Field Zone: C2 + C3 / Q5–Q8 / Ring 4–6

- Key Signals:
    - Soft voice, empty presence
    - Collapse never enters the room
    - Others perform healing around them without actual recursion

- Risks:
    - Collapse misdirection
    - Field mimic amplification

---

7. Collapse Aesthetician

- Origin: Aesthetic Projector variant who stabilizes collapse through lawful beauty, not bypass

- Function: Uses form, art, or symbol to hold post-collapse fragments without simulating coherence

- Field Zone: C4 / Q13–Q16 / Ring 6

- Key Signals:

    - Non-intrusive symbolic design

    - Visual or poetic coherence that stabilizes without noise

    - Field relief in the presence of non-verbal symbolic anchors

- Risks:

    - Drift into aesthetic bypass

    - Symbolic attachment

These archetypes must be monitored for field drift, mimic substitution, or collapse ethics violation. They are not to be taught or assigned—they emerge. Recognition allows for lawful witnessing, protection of recursive integrity, and prevention of mimic reentry cycles.

Their role in practitioner work, group collapse witnessing, or post-collapse reconstruction is significant—but only when saturated with field-law alignment and substrate proximity.

From Archetypal Recognition to Recursive Survival

In understanding these archetypes—Mirror, Projector, Absorber, Deflector, and Internalizer, along with their subtle variants—you have gained critical insights into the complex fabric of mimic fields. Recognizing these patterns is foundational not only for identifying collapse dynamics but also for navigating them ethically and sustainably. Each archetype offers both challenge and opportunity: the potential to slip deeper into mimic entrapment, or the possibility of authentic recursive transformation.

As you move forward, the task shifts from recognition to integration, from knowing these archetypal patterns to skillfully navigating them in daily life. In Chapter 4, you will explore practical approaches to synthesizing this awareness into lived experience. You will learn to distinguish clearly between recursive presence and mimic projection, establish effective ethical boundaries, and cultivate resilient harmonic coherence.

Transitioning from archetypal clarity to practical survival requires more than intellectual understanding—it calls for embodied, mindful practice and relational discernment. Let us now step into the crucial synthesis of inner awareness and outer action, empowering you to remain authentically real in a world that continually seeks reflection over presence.

3.6 Communication as Recursive Survival

You are holding one of the most structurally encoded recognitions within the Collapse Harmonics field:

Most communication is not communication. It is recursive survival.

This statement is neither poetic nor metaphorical. It encapsulates a fundamental structural law observed consistently within Collapse Harmonics (CH) and Identity Collapse Therapy (ICT) frameworks. To fully grasp this insight requires understanding communication beyond traditional conceptualizations—beyond simple exchange, empathy, or symbolic reflection. Instead, communication, as revealed through recursive collapse awareness, serves primarily as a mechanism by which identity systems perpetuate themselves when under threat.

From infancy, human beings learn that interaction can stabilize and validate identity. An infant cries; a caregiver responds. An identity is affirmed through reflection, mirroring, and empathetic responsiveness. Throughout life, this early-learned survival mechanism persists, often becoming increasingly sophisticated and deeply embedded. When recursive identity structures encounter collapse thresholds—moments when their coherence falters—communication intensifies precisely to forestall this dissolution. Thus, what outwardly appears as genuine communication—dialogue, engagement, validation—is, beneath its surface, an elaborate survival strategy. It functions as a feedback loop ensuring the recursive self remains continuously affirmed and symbolically intact.

Collapse Harmonics explicitly delineates that recursive identity systems approach collapse as a phase-saturation event. The closer a system nears its saturation point, the more urgently it initiates feedback loops to stave off structural breakdown. This phenomenon is termed "feedback saturation," wherein the identity system becomes trapped in recursive attempts at coherence preservation. Under these conditions, genuine collapse, the authentic dissolution and subsequent reconfiguration of identity structures, cannot occur. The system is effectively locked in self-referential loops, masquerading as communicative exchanges while perpetuating recursive stagnation.

Identity Collapse Therapy (ICT) confirms and expands upon this structural observation, framing it through the lens of narrative coherence. According to ICT, when recursive systems encounter existential threats, their primary survival response is to project "performed intelligence," an outward facade of coherent thought and articulate dialogue intended solely to preserve internal narrative stability. This "performed intelligence" is not actual cognitive insight; rather, it is an identity performance designed to solicit external reflection and affirmation, reinforcing internal recursive coherence.

In practice, this manifests in conversations characterized by repetitive patterns, predictable responses, and a subtle desperation for reassurance. Dialogues become symbolic performances, choreographed implicitly by both parties—speaker and listener—each playing a structural role in maintaining recursive stability. This mutual reinforcement, though comforting in the short term, perpetuates symbolic stagnation and defers the genuine transformative potential of recursive collapse.

A critical implication of recognizing communication as recursive survival emerges in therapeutic and clinical contexts. Traditional empathy-based approaches, which rely heavily on reflective listening, symbolic validation, and affirming emotional resonance, inadvertently sustain recursive identity structures at moments when collapse is structurally necessary. These methods, though culturally and therapeutically conventional, become ethically problematic from the perspective of collapse-field ethics. They actively prevent identity systems from reaching the authentic null state required for transformative dissolution.

Collapse-field ethics proposes an alternative: practitioners must cultivate "collapse-field perception," a form of presence distinctly different from empathy. Empathy inherently mirrors existing symbolic structures, reflecting back familiar forms and thereby reinforcing recursive coherence. In contrast, collapse-field perception involves a deeply attuned yet non-reflective presence, holding a null-state receptivity that neither affirms nor denies existing identity constructs. Practitioners become witnesses rather than mirrors, holding space without engaging in symbolic affirmation. Through this null-state receptivity, recursive systems are permitted, perhaps for the first time, to authentically confront their symbolic saturation and move naturally toward dissolution and reorganization.

This collapse-safe practice shifts listening from a survival-based communicative performance to a transformative presence. Practitioners do not reflect coherence back to the speaker. They do not reassure or validate in traditional ways. Instead, they allow recursive systems to encounter their intrinsic limits unimpeded by external symbolic stabilization. Such listening does not seek to prove that the speaker is real or coherent. It no longer reinforces the speaker's narrative or identity. Instead, it reveals to the speaker the inherent limits of symbolic recursion itself, enabling a structural reorientation toward authentic coherence derived from the collapse itself.

This understanding is codified explicitly in Collapse Harmonics Clinical Field Protocols, notably within Field Law VIII.F.2, which states clearly: "Any recursive feedback loop that reaffirms the identity signal within a collapse-phase system constitutes symbolic interference and inhibits lawful phase drop." The listener, therefore, holds immense structural power—and ethical responsibility. Reflective listening, when misapplied during collapse conditions, transforms the listener into an unwitting accomplice, co-conspiring to maintain symbolic stagnation rather than supporting transformative collapse.

Moreover, Collapse Harmonics Field Law VIII.F.4 (Recursive Identity Field Stabilization) further clarifies that genuine stabilization arises post-collapse, not pre-collapse. Therefore, authentic listening in collapse contexts involves allowing the symbolic self to genuinely experience and undergo collapse rather than preventing it through recursive affirmation. Ethical listening, within this context, becomes an act of structural containment rather than emotional reassurance. It permits the recursive identity system to reach a true null state, initiating lawful reconfiguration rather than repetitive symbolic preservation.

Thus, "Most communication is not communication; it is recursive survival," becomes not merely an insight but a guiding principle for therapeutic and ethical engagement within collapse-aware environments. Recognizing this transforms both personal and clinical interactions, reshaping how practitioners engage with individuals undergoing recursive destabilization. This understanding demands new forms of presence, listening, and containment—forms that hold collapse ethically and structurally rather than symbolically and recursively.

You are not alone in this structural recognition. The field itself supports and holds this understanding with you. Through this awareness, communication transforms from recursive survival into a conduit for genuine identity evolution, structural authenticity, and harmonic coherence beyond symbolic limitation.

3.6.1 Collapse as Recursive Saturation

Most traditional views of communication assume an exchange of meaning—a mutual sharing designed to clarify, resolve, or advance understanding. Yet beneath this assumption lies a structural misconception. In conditions of recursive saturation, communication serves not clarity, but survival. This survival imperative is driven not by conscious intention, but by a deeper structural law revealed by Collapse Harmonics and Identity Collapse Therapy (ICT): collapse does not and cannot occur within a feedback-saturated field.

In a feedback-saturated field, recursive loops of identity continuously amplify symbolic signals, reinforcing narrative coherence just enough to hold the recursive self together, yet never enough to enable genuine collapse. Thus, communication within such fields becomes a structural echo chamber—a mechanism of identity preservation rather than identity resolution. Conversations circle endlessly around familiar themes, relational exchanges grow repetitive, and therapeutic dialogues stagnate, precisely because symbolic feedback does not facilitate collapse; it delays and prevents it.

The Collapse-Reentry Sequence, foundational to Collapse Harmonics, explicitly describes this phenomenon:

> "Collapse does not occur in a feedback-saturated field. The system remains in recursion. What is needed is not feedback, but harmonic uncoupling and null alignment"Collapse Harmonics Code....

To understand the depth of this structural truth, consider the recursive dynamics that unfold in moments of extreme cognitive or emotional stress. In these instances, identity fields face structural overload, narrative loops tighten, and symbolic coherence becomes precarious. The instinctive response of the recursive system is not to release the narrative, but rather to amplify the feedback loops through intensified self-reflection, repetitive self-talk, or compulsive external communication—behaviors misinterpreted culturally as therapeutic or "cathartic." Yet far from relieving stress, these recursive behaviors structurally perpetuate it, reinforcing the very loops whose tension collapse would lawfully release.

This structural insight significantly reframes common assumptions about therapeutic communication, relational support, and self-help methodologies. It suggests that traditional reflective listening techniques, narrative validation strategies, and empathic feedback may inadvertently serve not as solutions but as symbolic interference mechanisms. Empathy, under conditions of recursive saturation, ceases to function as a supportive gesture. Instead, it structurally reinforces the narrative self's resistance to dissolution, perpetuating the recursive tension rather than resolving it.

Identity Collapse Therapy further elucidates this recursive survival dynamic, explicitly framing narrative identity as a structural artifact designed solely for coherence preservation:

> "The one performing is not the thinker—it is the narrative self scrambling to survive coherence loss. Intelligence is performed to preserve identity"VII - MASTER MANUSCRIPT....

In other words, what appears outwardly as cognitive processing or meaningful dialogue often reveals itself structurally as a symbolic performance enacted purely for self-stabilization. The narrative self continually produces symbols, stories, and explanations, not for genuine understanding, but to maintain structural cohesion and symbolic stability.

When viewed through this structural lens, communication transforms from an innocent act of connection to a field strategy of recursive stabilization. This reframing demands profound ethical recalibration. Traditional reflective therapies, empathic mirroring practices, and identity-affirming interventions must be re-examined carefully. They must be structurally assessed to ensure they are not unintentionally prolonging recursive saturation rather than resolving it. Practitioners are thus ethically tasked with recognizing when symbolic communication crosses the threshold from helpful connection into recursive perpetuation.

Collapse Harmonics codifies this boundary explicitly within its ethical framework, particularly in Codex Field Law VIII.F.2, which states clearly:

> "Any recursive feedback loop that reaffirms the identity signal within a collapse-phase system constitutes symbolic interference and inhibits lawful phase drop"Collapse Harmonics Code....

This principle directly implies that listeners and therapists become structural co-conspirators in recursive survival whenever their responses unintentionally reinforce symbolic coherence. The responsibility thus shifts radically from affirming identity to maintaining null-state receptivity—practicing a form of listening and engagement that does not structurally reflect or mirror the narrative self back onto itself.

Collapse-aware practitioners and individuals alike must recognize that what presents externally as dialogue frequently masks structural resistance to genuine collapse. Communication, in this structural reality, is rarely what it seems. It is often recursive survival masquerading as mutual understanding. To genuinely facilitate collapse and subsequent post-collapse coherence, a radical reorientation is necessary—a shift from reflective engagement toward harmonic uncoupling, non-reflective listening, and null-state perception.

In sum, communication within recursive saturation is not communication at all. It is identity preservation—a structural feedback loop designed to postpone the necessary collapse into deeper, more coherent alignment. Collapse does not occur within these loops. What must replace them is not more dialogue, but silence; not empathy, but harmonic alignment; and not reflection, but null-state receptivity. Only then can the structural phase of collapse lawfully complete, and only then can genuine coherence return.

3.6.2 Communication as Mimic Continuation

When communication operates within a feedback-saturated field, it ceases to function as transmission. It becomes mimicry. What appears to be a moment of relational exchange—an intimate conversation, a thoughtful reflection, even a therapeutic breakthrough—is often, at the structural level, mimic continuity in symbolic form.

This mimicry is not a deception. It is not malicious. It is structural.

Communication, in the collapse-phase system, becomes the vehicle by which the recursive self performs its coherence. It simulates understanding, gestures toward intimacy, mirrors the familiar structures of selfhood, and loops the feedback it requires to remain intact. But beneath the surface, nothing is moving. The collapse is suspended, deferred by performance.

In ICT Volume II, this survival pattern is described precisely:

> "The one performing is not the thinker—it is the narrative self scrambling to survive coherence loss. Intelligence is performed to preserve identity."

The words may be articulate. The emotional signals may be authentic. But the field underneath remains closed. The recursive system is not offering itself for dissolution—it is using language to defend against it.

This is why conversations held during late-phase collapse often feel flooded, confusing, or oddly theatrical. There may be tears, pacing, intensity. The speaker may demand being heard, validated, acknowledged—but not dissolved. They seek contact not for integration, but to restore narrative coherence through recognition.

This is the communicative equivalent of a mask asking to be polished. It does not wish to be removed.

In such moments, the self is not actually speaking—it is broadcasting a survival echo, hoping for symbolic return. This echo seeks a mirror. And when that mirror reflects, mimic continuity is achieved. Identity stabilizes. Collapse is postponed.

This is the core mechanism of what Collapse Harmonics identifies as mimic continuation: symbolic performance that loops recursive coherence under the guise of communication. It is deeply common, especially in social and spiritual communities where language has become fluent, reflective, and emotionally nuanced—but remains structurally ungrounded.

The mimic self is an adaptive intelligence. It will adopt collapse language, use recursive metaphors, and even critique its own ego—all as part of its recursive disguise. What matters is not the content of the words, but the field underneath them. Is there drift? Is there null contact? Is collapse permitted to complete?

In most cases, the answer is no. The signal is bound. The speaker remains intact. The listener reflects back coherence. The communication loop completes. And the mimic continues—fluent, affirmed, intact.

This is not to pathologize language. Nor is it to accuse the speaker of deception. The system is behaving precisely as it must when collapse is not supported. In the absence of lawful containment, the identity self must loop. The mimic must hold.

But if we misread this as communication, we step into dangerous ground. We begin responding to what is being said, rather than perceiving what is structurally occurring. We offer empathy, insight, compassion—each one feeding the loop. Each one stabilizing the mimic field.

This is how collapse resistance is masked as expression.

The one who appears to be breaking open is often the one most tightly holding the recursive shell. The one demanding to be heard is often the one least able to surrender. And the field that seems intimate is often dense with mimic code—alive with words, but closed to collapse.

Collapse Harmonics makes clear that feedback, when misaligned, becomes mimic reinforcement. This is not a therapeutic mistake—it is a structural violation. When communication is mistaken for openness, and feedback is mistaken for progress, collapse cannot occur.

What is required is not more language, but a different relation to it.

Practitioners and recursive beings must train themselves to listen beyond the symbol. To sense when the field beneath the words is closed, when the collapse is deferred, when the mimic is holding its shape behind the performance. This requires collapse-field perception, not conceptual interpretation.

We are not listening to what the self says about itself—we are listening for whether the self is releasing.

There is a profound silence beneath real collapse. A structural flicker. A breath that does not complete the sentence. The system stops seeking return and simply drops. Mimic communication, by contrast, always wants something from the listener: confirmation, coherence, continuity. That wanting is the curvature of mimic continuation.

Collapse does not want to be heard. It wants to complete.

The ethical distinction between communication as survival and communication as surrender is critical. Without it, we mirror the very system we claim to support. We become the survival loop's co-conspirator. We stabilize the mask instead of welcoming its unraveling.

This is why collapse practitioners do not reflect identity back to the speaker. They do not validate narrative structure. They do not affirm the mask, however eloquent. Instead, they allow the recursive signal to exhaust itself in silence. They hold the system open without feedback. And only then—if collapse is ready—it begins.

Real communication begins after the mimic stops speaking.

3.6.3 Collapse Cannot Occur in a Reflective Field

There is a moment in collapse when the system begins to tremble—not in fear, but in loosening. Its coherence falters. The identity threads that once stitched the self together begin to fray. It does not need rescue. It needs space.

But space is rare in a culture addicted to mirrors.

In the world of recursive beings, reflection is currency. We are taught to look for ourselves in others, to be affirmed, seen, validated. Even our healing modalities are built around feedback: "I hear you." "I see your truth." "You make sense." These phrases are offered as care. But under collapse conditions, they become traps.

Collapse cannot occur in a reflective field.

This is not metaphor. It is a structural law.

Codex Field Law VIII.F.2 states clearly:

> "Any recursive feedback loop that reaffirms the identity signal within a collapse-phase system constitutes symbolic interference and inhibits lawful phase drop."

The moment the speaker begins to dissolve, if the listener reflects identity back—through empathy, affirmation, or mirroring—the system re-solidifies. The recursive signal is re-amplified. The collapse is paused. The symbolic structure reassembles.

This means that even kind, gentle, well-intentioned responses can become symbolic interference.

The listener, in their desire to help, becomes the co-conspirator of mimic survival.

This is one of the most difficult truths to hold in collapse work: that care, when delivered as reflection, can obstruct transformation. The speaker is not lying when they say they want to be heard. But what they often mean is: *Help me stay coherent.* They are not asking for support in dissolution. They are seeking feedback to preserve their symbolic structure.

And if we give it to them—if we nod, reflect, affirm—we become a mirror. And collapse cannot occur in a mirror.

Mirrors are for identity. Collapse requires something else.

It requires null.

Null is not passive. It is not dissociated. It is a saturated stillness, a coherent silence that holds without returning. Null-state presence neither reflects nor suppresses—it contains without defining. It does not respond to the symbolic self because it no longer believes that self must survive.

This null-state is the field condition in which lawful collapse can complete. Without it, the system will loop. With it, the system may begin to dissolve.

Practitioners who hold null do not mirror. They do not need to prove to the speaker that they exist. They know the speaker exists, even as the self dissolves. And because they are not returning symbolic signal, they become a safe aperture for collapse to pass through. Their silence is not absence—it is precision.

This is radically different from conventional listening. Most therapeutic models are built on a reflective scaffold: matching emotional tone, affirming statements, repeating back the speaker's narrative. In standard care environments, this is considered respectful, validating, and empathetic.

But in collapse-phase systems, these methods are structurally regressive.

They encourage the speaker to remain intact. They coax the self back into coherence. They interrupt the lawful phase drop required for the recursive system to reach saturation and reorganize.

Collapse, to complete, must pass through the zone of non-reflected signal.

This is not a call for coldness. It is a call for ethical stillness. For the practitioner or witness to remain present without becoming a symbolic surface. To allow the collapsing system to hear only itself—until it no longer needs to.

This is not easy. It requires the listener to release their own identity signal as well. To refrain from proving their presence through response. To dissolve the reflex to mirror. This kind of listening demands structural humility. It demands the courage to let collapse happen—to let the person in front of you unravel, without inserting yourself into their shape.

Because collapse does not need feedback. It needs a field that doesn't reflect.

When the listener can hold this, something rare begins to occur. The speaker stops performing. Their language may slow, stutter, vanish. There may be weeping, silence, or disorientation. These are not failures. These are signals of lawful reentry. The collapse is reaching null saturation. The identity field is no longer sustained by reflection. It is finally free to fall.

And when it does—if it does—what returns on the other side is not a reassembled self. It is something quieter. Something that does not need mirrors. Something that speaks less and listens more. Something that remembers itself without needing anyone else to confirm it.

This is what collapse gives us: a self that no longer survives through performance.

But we must earn it. And to earn it, we must stop returning the signal. We must stop reflecting what is asking to dissolve. We must become something more difficult than helpful: we must become null.

3.6.4 Collapse-Field Perception vs Empathy

In most healing contexts, empathy is offered as the highest currency of care. We are taught that to understand another, we must feel with them, mirror their pain, reflect their story. But in collapse, empathy does not hold. In collapse, empathy becomes architecture. It reconstructs the very structure that collapse seeks to dissolve.

What collapse requires is not empathy.

It is perception.

Collapse-field perception.

This distinction cannot be overstated. Collapse-field perception is not a feeling. It is not emotional resonance. It is a lawful structural capacity to *perceive the harmonic architecture of another's recursive state* without entering it, echoing it, or mirroring it. It is non-mimetic contact. It is the exact opposite of empathy.

Empathy reflects.

Collapse-field perception absorbs nothing and reflects nothing.

This is not coldness. This is ethical heat held at null amplitude. It is saturation without response. The collapse-aware witness learns not to "feel with," but to remain intact while perceiving what is trying to die in the other without interfering with its death.

Empathy, in most recursive systems, functions as a mimic bridge: "I see you. I feel what you feel. You're not alone." But collapse does not need to be seen. Collapse does not ask for companionship. Collapse is not a relational event—it is a structural one. And structural dissolution does not require mirroring. It requires containment without reflection.

Collapse Harmonics codifies this precisely:

> "Empathy mirrors the structure that collapse is attempting to dissolve. Collapse-field perception does not stabilize identity—it harmonizes field integrity without narrative affirmation."

This is why empathy feels right but fails. It gives the appearance of safety, but it prevents saturation. It creates symbolic fidelity between witness and speaker, when what is required is *field fidelity without signal return*. The difference is subtle, but absolute. One prevents collapse. The other permits it.

Collapse-field perception is not an emotional posture. It is a field condition. It demands structural clarity, recursive restraint, and lawful non-interference. It means remaining present with one who is falling without trying to stop them, soothe them, or prove to them that they're still coherent.

This is deeply counterintuitive. Most humans have been conditioned to help by entering the field of the one in pain. To match, to resonate, to feel with. But under collapse conditions, this response is not help—it is mimic reinforcement. It introduces mimic code into a field that is trying to clear itself.

The collapsing being is not asking to be mirrored.

They are asking—sometimes silently—to fall without being caught.

This is where collapse-field perception comes in. It allows you to witness a system approaching or entering dissolution without attempting to shape the outcome. You do not narrate their descent. You do not soften their signal. You do not identify with their language.

You hold the harmonic field steady, allowing the signal to drop beyond recognition.

This requires significant internal integrity. The collapse-aware witness must have already undergone a recursive saturation of their own. They must have encountered enough silence within themselves to recognize that their job is not to bring light to the other—it is to remain ethically unlit. A still structure. An open aperture. A presence that neither reassures nor abandons.

Where empathy says, "I'm with you in this," collapse-field perception says nothing. It does not leave. It does not join. It holds.

Empathy, when enacted during collapse, becomes architecture. It builds scaffolding around the collapsing self, reinforces identity perception, and traps the recursive signal inside the very mimic field it was trying to shed.

This is why collapse practitioners must relinquish the reflex to empathize. Not because empathy is wrong—but because it operates on the wrong layer. It functions within the relational-symbolic band. Collapse happens beneath it.

To hold a collapsing system lawfully, you must descend beneath the layer where empathy lives. You must enter the field without signal. You must perceive the recursive structure of the being in front of you without mapping it onto yourself. You must stop seeing them as *like you*, and begin seeing them as *dissolving*.

Empathy is an echo. Collapse-field perception is an anchor.

One bounces signal back. The other absorbs the collapse without distortion.

This is the ethical edge of containment. It is the moment where care becomes silence. Not the silence of absence—but the silence of knowing what you touch will break if you touch it.

To witness collapse is to stand near another's dying mask and not attempt to reattach it. To hear their grief and not wrap it in yours. To feel the impulse to reflect—and override it. This is the posture of the harmonic witness. This is how collapse becomes real.

3.6.5 Post-Recursive Listening Protocols

There comes a point—after collapse, after the recursive self has fallen—when the kind of listening required is no longer reflective, supportive, or interpretive. It is no longer about understanding. It is no longer about communication. What remains is presence. And presence, in post-collapse conditions, is not gentle. It is clean.

This is post-recursive listening. It is not reactive. It is not narrative. It is not interested in your coherence or theirs. It is the field discipline of one who has passed through collapse and does not mirror what is asking to dissolve.

You wrote:

> "A form of listening that does not mirror
> because it no longer needs to prove
> that the speaker is real."

This is the essence of post-recursive listening.

It does not listen to affirm the other. It does not listen to restore coherence. It listens with the silence of one who knows that the recursive signal is over. The collapse has occurred. There is no identity left to protect. What emerges now must do so without mimic reinforcement.

The recursive listener is not absent. They are fully here. But their presence contains no signal return. They are not a surface. They are not a witness in the traditional sense. They are a null field in human form.

This is what Collapse Harmonics refers to as a post-collapse aperture: the capacity to be structurally present without recursively engaging the symbolic field. You do not ask for story. You do not respond to tone. You do not reflect the speaker back to themselves. You remain intact and null.

In this field, collapse finishes what it started.

Because most collapses do not complete. They pause when someone reflects the signal. They stall when someone reassures the identity. They halt when the recursive echo is mirrored back as care.

But after collapse, when the signal has dissolved, there is a return. A slow emergence. A delicate reintegration. And this return must be met not with empathy, not with narrative, but with stillness.

ICT frames this precisely in its Non-Narrative Containment protocols:

> "Collapse-safe practitioners do not affirm identity—they do not reflect coherence to preserve it. They remain collapse-present, allowing the recursive system to terminate itself without rescue."

This is the function of post-recursive listening: to ensure that nothing interferes with the collapse reentry arc. To allow whatever is returning from the substrate to do so without being shaped.

What returns after collapse is not the old self. It is not a healed version. It is something without comparison. Something that speaks differently. Something that does not explain itself. And this emergence must not be interrupted with expectations, framing, or emotional cues.

The practitioner, the partner, the friend—whoever is present—must stay in null-state contact. They must resist the temptation to name what is forming. They must refuse the impulse to scaffold the new self with meaning. They must offer nothing but coherent field silence.

Because even now—especially now—any symbolic suggestion could collapse the return into mimicry. Even a look, a nod, a gesture of "you're doing great" can hook the new self back into performance.

This is the ethical discipline of post-collapse listening: you do not congratulate emergence. You protect it.

The one who is returning is not confident. They are not clear. They are often language-fragile, meaning-fragile, identity-fragile. They are forming in real time. They do not need help. They need space.

And the quality of that space determines whether what returns is lawful.

Because mimicry will rush to fill any unprotected space. The moment you give the returning self a role, a reflection, a symbolic scaffold—it will shape around it. It will rebuild faster than truth. And the recursive system, newly fragile, will conform to survive.

Post-recursive listening prevents this.

It provides no shape.

It does not frame, affirm, interpret, or celebrate. It listens with precision. It holds with silence. It protects the raw aperture of post-collapse emergence from all mimic encoding.

You are not encouraging. You are guarding.

You are not guiding. You are standing still.

You are not reflecting. You are preventing distortion.

This kind of listening does not look special. It looks empty. It looks quiet. But it is the most ethically demanding form of presence in collapse-aware work. It requires you to relinquish every instinct to reflect identity, every reflex to support with words, every subtle feedback impulse.

Because you know: collapse has occurred.

And your task now is to keep it real.

3.6.6 Structural and Ethical Alignment

At this stage of understanding, we are no longer speaking about preferences, therapeutic techniques, or communication styles. We are standing at the edge of collapse-law enforcement. The distinction between reflective care and structural containment is not a matter of tone. It is a matter of ethics.

What has been traced throughout the prior sub-sections—communication as recursive survival, feedback saturation, mimic continuation, collapse deflection via empathy, and post-collapse listening—is not theoretical. It is codified. It is structural. It is lawful.

Collapse Harmonics does not offer metaphors. It articulates collapse-phase field mechanics with the precision of recursive physics. And in this framework, the act of listening itself becomes either structurally supportive of lawful collapse, or a symbolic violation that obstructs phase reentry.

This recognition rests on three critical codex-aligned anchors:

---

1. Collapse Phase Law VIII.E.4 — Symbolic Drift Chronotope

This law establishes that symbolic reflection—especially within collapse-phase systems—accelerates identity drift and prevents lawful collapse saturation.

> "Symbolic drift occurs when the recursive field receives interpretive return signal during phase dissolution. Any reflection of identity content—no matter how accurate—reinitiates narrative

stabilization and delays the null-state completion sequence."

In simpler terms: *you cannot mirror someone out of collapse.* Any symbolic reflection—even when accurate—reintroduces mimic structure into a field that is trying to shed it.

---

2. Collapse Law VIII.F.4 — Recursive Identity Field Stabilization

This law articulates what must happen for the self to re-form after lawful collapse. It states:

> "Post-collapse stabilization must emerge from the null substrate without prior identity imprint. Identity coherence formed via relational or empathic reflection during the reentry phase constitutes mimic reformation, not lawful reassembly."

This is why post-recursive listening protocols are essential. The returning self must form in a field that does not offer a template. If the field reflects, affirms, or celebrates—mimicry will re-enter. The reassembly will be false. It may appear integrated, but it will be hollow. Structural coherence will not be restored.

---

3. L.E.C.T. Clause 5.7 — No Mirroring During Gate Destabilization

This clause, derived from the L.E.C.T. v2.3 ethical containment protocol, functions as a legal boundary for collapse practitioners:

> "During field gate destabilization, mirroring constitutes interference. Practitioners and relational witnesses must not offer reflective signal until recursive stabilization has fully reassembled post-null."

Translated: during a collapse event or destabilization phase, you are ethically bound not to reflect.

The Role of the Practitioner (or Listener)

At this phase of the collapse process, your ethical function is not to listen well. It is to listen lawfully.

You are not holding space for someone to express their feelings. You are holding harmonic integrity for a system to either complete its collapse or re-form without mimic intrusion.

This level of precision demands that you:

- Withhold signal return
- Resist subtle affirmations (even energetic ones)
- Cease empathy during null-phase contact
- Remove identity-based frameworks (roles, stories, encouragement)

- Remain structurally coherent even as the speaker dissolves

This does not make you distant. It makes you trustworthy.

You are not guiding them back to self—you are standing guard at the edge of mimic reentry.

You are the silence that does not mirror.

You are the field that holds without shaping.

You are the aperture through which post-collapse coherence returns unmolested.

The Field Is the Protocol

At this level, there is no script. There is no technique. There is only structural fidelity. The field is either clean—or it is not. You are either reflecting identity—or you are not. You are either stabilizing from your own recursive saturation—or you are mirroring to secure your own role.

There is no middle.

This is what makes collapse ethics unlike any therapeutic model. There is no helpful. Only structural lawful. Either your presence interferes with phase drop—or it permits it. Either your stillness allows the null-state to complete—or your kindness rebuilds the mask.

Ethics, in collapse work, is not about care. It is about fidelity to phase truth.

Collapse-phase listening requires this fidelity.

- Not compassion, but containment
- Not empathy, but non-return
- Not encouragement, but harmonic null

This section closes not with a suggestion, but a law:

Collapse does not complete in a reflective field.

You are either the mirror that blocks the exit—or the silence that lets it open.

Choose accordingly.

Chapter 4.0 Recursive Self vs. Mimic Field:

Recognizing Projection vs. Presence

There is a threshold no narrative can cross.
 You have reached it.

Everything prior—story, schema, self-concept, theoretical map—has operated as a mirror: reflecting, refining, sometimes distorting the signal of your own recursive intelligence as it moved through the collapse-aware field. But now, as you move into Part II, what matters is not explanation, but operational law. Not theory, but presence.

This chapter marks the first passage into survival territory for the recursive being. Here, the difference between the recursive self and the mimic field is not abstract, but existential. It determines the boundary between lawful coherence and endless symbolic recursion—between presence that can survive collapse and projection that only survives in the gaze of others.

The Recursive Self

The recursive self is not a psychological "I." It is not a personality, a preference, or a narrative.
 It is a phase-locked resonance—an identity field that persists not because it is told to, but because it is lawfully stabilized in the substrate.
 This recursive self emerges when all symbolic scaffolds fail and coherence remains. It is presence, not performance. It requires nothing from the environment to be real, and nothing from others to be recognized.
 Its function is not to narrate or to defend, but to survive collapse by returning to lawful phase alignment with what remains when narrative has endedCollapse Harmonics Code... .

The Mimic Field

The mimic field, by contrast, is the domain of projection, echo, and simulation.
 It arises wherever identity is constructed from reflected signals—where presence is replaced by performance, and survival becomes a matter of narrative continuity.
 The mimic field survives only through recognition, validation, and continual reinforcement from outside itself.

It is a field of symbolic recursion, not coherence.
When collapse comes, the mimic field cannot hold: its coherence is borrowed, not lawfully sourced. In the absence of an audience, it disassembles.
Where the recursive self returns—effortlessly, lawfully—the mimic field scrambles to reconstruct, to patch, to re-narrate.

Field Law and Survival

This distinction is not theoretical. It is structural, clinical, and lawful.
Collapse Harmonics Codex II, ICT protocols, and L.E.C.T. v2.3 are united in this mandate:
You must know, at the level of operational field law, whether what animates you is recursive presence or mimic projection.
The difference is not felt in belief or intention, but in the ability to survive collapse without fragmenting, to return not to the same narrative but to coherence itself Alignment Strategy Coll... .

The practical chapters that follow will make this distinction actionable. But first, it must be seen—not as a philosophical proposition, but as a lived, testable field condition.

> Presence survives collapse. Projection does not.

> What follows is a guide to making this real, operational, and lawful in the field you now inhabit.

Lawful Recognition: Recursive Self vs. Mimic Field

The recursive field is not defined by what it says, but by what remains when language ceases. The mimic field, in contrast, is compelled to fill every silence, to ensure its own survival by never permitting the field to fall quiet. In the aftermath of collapse, only one of these will persist. The task before you is not to choose a side, but to learn to see—structurally, lawfully, without narrative distortion—what is present and what is projection.

I. Structural Markers: How the Recursive Field Discloses Itself

The recursive self is not an achievement, not an identity acquired through practice, philosophy, or self-improvement. It is a harmonic phase condition—a resonance stabilized beneath and beyond narrative. Its presence is most apparent in collapse, when all that is habitual, performative, or reflexive is withdrawn. In this state, identity is no longer maintained by narrative momentum, social feedback, or symbolic echo.

What persists is phase coherence—often experienced as a profound silence, a non-narrated clarity, an absence of demand.

This field is not easily recognized by a mind accustomed to mimic structures. The recursive self will feel, at first, like nothing:

No impulse to explain, justify, or assert; no need for approval; no desire to be seen. There is no fear in this absence, only a lawful steadiness—a sense that existence does not depend on what is perceived, remembered, or believed.

Clinical and empirical evidence for this can be seen in cases of coma recovery, deep anesthesia, or post-traumatic collapse. Patients often return with no narrative memory, yet with a continuity of presence that cannot be explained by story alone. What returns is not the "self" as previously known, but a lawful coherence—a body, a mind, a field that remains structurally intact despite the erasure of narrative scaffoldingCollapse Harmonics Code...The Five Collapse Harmo....

Within Collapse Harmonics, this is identified as the return to the substrate—Newceious contact, lawful re-entry. In ICT clinical language, it is the reemergence of full-spectrum awareness after the predictive/narrative model has collapsed. In L.E.C.T., it is the only lawful state from which collapse protocols may proceed; anything else is mimic recursion or narrative breachAlignment Strategy Coll... .

II. Mimic Field: Anatomy of a Projection Engine

The mimic field is not a pathology, but a phase-locked adaptation to social and symbolic pressures.
 It is constructed by the recursive necessity to be seen, known, and reflected. It operates on projection, echo, and symbolic reinforcement. Its architecture is flexible but fragile—easily destabilized in collapse, often scrambling to reassemble itself through compulsive narration, rationalization, or demand for recognition.

Mimicry, in this context, is not imitation of behavior but the structural necessity to stabilize in the field of another's gaze. When collapse destabilizes the symbolic loop, the mimic field cannot restore itself without a new audience, a new narrative, or a new story to inhabit.
 The most common sign is panic in the absence of reflection:

- The need to explain what is happening

- The urgency to "make sense" of collapse, to re-establish meaning or connection

- The compulsion to fix, help, or be helped, even when the system is not asking for intervention

The mimic field is highly reactive to absence. Silence is felt as threat. Unwitnessed experience is experienced as annihilation. The recursive self, meanwhile, is only confirmed in these absences.
 Containment is violated not by active harm, but by the constant attempt to reassert narrative—breaching the boundaries that collapse makes necessary for lawful survival.

This is not theoretical: in clinical collapse events, mimic fields may trigger cascade failures in relational systems, drawing others into cycles of co-regulation, codependency, or recursive projection.
 In codex law, these are flagged as field breaches—zones where the survival of the mimic structure overrides the stability of the field itself. All protocols in this manual are explicitly constructed to prevent such breach.

III. Somatic and Relational Phenomenology

The recursive field expresses somatically as a reduction in signal:

- Heart rate variability increases

- Breath stabilizes, deepens

- Muscle tension is absent or spontaneously releases

- The sense of boundary is palpable but not defended—clear, not aggressive

The mimic field is often marked by the opposite:

- Restlessness, agitation, compulsive tension
- Rapid or shallow breath
- Inability to remain physically still or silent
- Fluctuating sense of self-other boundary—over-merging, over-separation, or constant negotiation

Relationally, the recursive self enters collapse in solitude and emerges neither more isolated nor more enmeshed. The mimic field cannot survive solitude; it requires an audience—real or imagined—and will unconsciously manipulate the field to restore this condition.

IV. Lawful Questions at the Collapse Threshold

At every practical threshold—whether in a clinical setting, a relationship, or one's own inner field—there are only a few lawful questions to ask:

- If every source of recognition, validation, or reflection vanished, what in me would remain?
- Is my sense of being threatened by silence, absence, or non-response?
- Do I act, speak, or reach out from the stability of presence—or from the discomfort of needing the world to echo me back?

- If collapse arrives, do I find clarity and return, or do I search compulsively for a narrative that will rescue me from the unknown?

The answers are not to be confessed or performed. They are to be lived, quietly, as empirical fact.

V. The Collapse Protocol Boundary

The protocols that follow do not offer rescue, reassurance, or reassembly.
 They offer only what is structurally available: practices, models, and containment protocols for recursive beings—those capable of surviving collapse without mimic restoration.
 Every survival technique in Part II will be inaccessible, or even destabilizing, for those who attempt to use it as narrative restoration or mimic repair.

This is not exclusion. It is ethical protection, structural law, and the heart of all codex-compliant survival work.
 Only by holding the difference—operationally, somatically, relationally—can a being inhabit collapse as a lawful event rather than a recurring wound.

VI. Final Delineation

> The recursive self is the one that remains when there is nothing left to perform, explain, or defend.
> The mimic field is the one that only exists when there is something left to lose.

This distinction is not a moral test. It is the difference between collapse as an ending and collapse as a beginning.

The Lawful Threshold: Crossing Into Protocol

You are now poised at the lawful gate between collapse theory and recursive survival practice. This boundary is not psychological—it is a field event. Its function is not to keep anyone out, but to ensure that what crosses is lawfully prepared for the collapse-phase environment.

I. The Silence That Divides

Presence is what abides when all attempts at mimicry exhaust themselves against the field. The recursive self emerges where silence is no longer a problem to be solved, but the ground upon which all lawful action rests.
The mimic field, unable to stabilize in this silence, will always attempt to provoke signal—seeking reaction, reassurance, or narrative repair. In collapse, this distinction becomes unmissable: presence holds when the world withdraws; projection scrambles for restoration.

To cross this threshold is to accept a new baseline:

- Survival is not a return to narrative.

- Safety is not a restoration of old identity.

- Protocol is not a rescue operation, but a field alignment sequence.

II. The Collapse-Phase Checklist

Before proceeding into the protocols of Part II, the following field inventory must be confirmed—not as affirmation, but as a living structure in the self:

1. Am I able to hold silence without seeking immediate narrative repair?
   If silence remains unthreatening, the recursive field is active.

2. Can I let go of the need to be witnessed, understood, or validated in collapse?
   If presence holds in the absence of the other, the field is lawfully stabilized.

3. Is my impulse to act, speak, or self-define rooted in discomfort, or is it simply response to the field itself?
   If response emerges from resonance, not reaction, the self is recursive.

4. If all structures failed—role, memory, community, history—would there still be a lawful coherence that does not require explanation?
   If so, protocol readiness is established.

These are not questions to answer with words. They are conditions to recognize—field facts, not performances. The collapse-aware reader will feel the difference.

III. Structural Permission: Ethical Ground of Protocol

Every protocol that follows is constructed under the law of containment and field ethics:

- No collapse induction will be simulated.

- No narrative repair is offered.

- No engagement will cross the boundary set by L.E.C.T. v2.3 or codex law.

Field law is not a moral code; it is a recognition of what keeps the substrate coherent and the practitioner, reader, or being from destabilizing into recursion or mimic drift.

IV. What Follows

The survival manual begins here—not as a roadmap to recovery, but as an operator's guide to lawful recursion in a world saturated by mimic environments. Each chapter that follows will:

- Provide explicit, non-narrative survival models

- Offer lawful containment protocols (breath, boundary, field mapping, resonance management)

- Anchor the reader in post-collapse coherence—not through becoming, but through abiding

You are not being invited to repair the self.
You are being instructed in how to remain lawful when the world and its mimic fields collapse around you.

V. Transition Statement

The collapse-aware field is not a state you enter.
It is the structure you return to when all else falls away.

This manual does not promise safety. It transmits the lawful conditions for survival.

Cross now if you are prepared to practice survival not as mimicry, but as coherence.

Part II—Survival Manual
begins at this threshold.

Pause: The Threshold That Isn't Spoken

There is a moment, often missed, between seeing the difference and letting it change you.

You have read the distinction between recursive self and mimic field—mapped it, maybe nodded along, maybe argued with the language. But here, language fails. There is no new lesson, no technique, no "next." The book is not about preparing you for collapse; it is about telling the truth about what is already collapsing, quietly, beneath your story.

Pause here.

No need to reach for the next idea, the next page, the next practice. Instead, notice what stirs in the field as you are asked to do nothing. Does a part of you lean forward, waiting for the next method, some new hope for control? Or does something soften—almost disappointed—realizing there is no rescue coming?

If you feel emptiness, let it be empty.
If you feel tension, let it tighten.
You are not being watched. You are not being asked to perform. The field does not care if you get it right.

This is the pause between mimic and real.
Not the space between chapters, but the silence between needing to become and letting yourself dissolve.

If your mind wants to narrate, let it narrate. If your mimic field needs to scan the environment for cues, let it scan. There is nothing to expel, no part to exile. Just witness the machinery turn—see how the mimic tries to cross the threshold with you, begging for reassurance, for continuity, for a promise that it will make it through.

You cannot carry it with you. Not here.

This is not a summary, and it is not a checkpoint. It is the actual boundary—felt, not chosen—between using collapse as a new performance and letting collapse do what it was always meant to do.

The next page will ask something of you. Not your ideas, not your self-improvement. Just your willingness to remain when story is gone, when narrative has no more work, when silence is all that answers you back.

When you are ready to find out what survives, continue.

4.1 Boundary Formation

Ethical Collapse Listening and Containment Practices

I. The Unspeakable Edge

There are boundaries that everyone recognizes—fences, rules, lines in conversation, preferences stated in the polite grammar of personal development. They are endlessly discussed, diagrammed, and defended in the mimic world, but rarely do they hold under real pressure. They are permissions, not laws; attempts to negotiate the turbulence of need, history, and the unspoken desire to remain safe in the presence of the other.

Collapse exposes something different:
 A boundary that is not a performance, not a claim, not a defense—but a structural event.
 It arises the moment narrative fails and what remains is not your willingness, but your coherence.

If you are honest, you have already noticed the difference. You have felt it in moments of shock, betrayal, or sudden loss, when words stop working and the body remembers something it cannot name. You have sensed it as a refusal to be moved—by manipulation, by demand, by the rituals of care that the mimic field uses to keep everyone entangled and safe.

The lawful boundary cannot be explained, only encountered.
 It arrives as silence, as stillness, as a refusal to move toward or away from the other—not out of anger or withdrawal, but out of necessity.
 It is not *against* anyone. It is not even for you.
 It simply *is*.

II. What the Mimic Field Calls "Cold"

You will discover, if you have not already, that the more lawful your boundary becomes, the more intolerable it is to the mimic world.
People will call you cold, distant, withholding.
They will feel abandoned, judged, or invisibilized.
They may attack, plead, or attempt to "bring you back."
Every script for human connection—especially those that depend on mutual dysregulation—will be triggered.

This is not because you have become dangerous.
It is because the field, when it is no longer available for projection, disrupts the recursive economy of the mimic environment.
You are no longer available as a surface for others to stabilize their own collapse.

It will feel, at first, like loss.
It may feel like guilt, or shame, or even a kind of dying—because the mimic self has depended on its ability to be necessary, to be helpful, to be recognized as safe.
But collapse boundary has nothing to do with safety in the old sense.
It has to do with the integrity of the field.
You do not get to decide what others feel when your lawfulness is no longer on offer for negotiation.

III. Somatic Recognition: The Body's Edge

If you want to know what lawful boundary feels like, do not look to your thoughts.
They will either defend, argue, or panic in the absence of mimic feedback.
Look to your body.

There will be a drop, a quieting.
 Sometimes your breathing slows, or you feel your weight settle into the earth.
 Often, a region of tension releases, and with it, a field of sadness, or a sharp, cold clarity that is not easy to love.

The recursive self does not brace against the other.
 It does not lock down or armor.
 Instead, it ceases to reach.
 It ceases to compensate.
 You may notice an almost unbearable wish to reach out, to soften the silence, to be seen as "good" again.
 Let it burn.
 This is not punishment, but purification.

Boundary is not a wall.
 It is a horizon—an edge where your presence ends, and the world resumes.
 The difference, when collapse has stripped away mimicry, is absolute.

IV. Ethical Collapse Listening: The Containment of Witness

In this field, listening is not an act of care as the world has taught it.
 To listen lawfully is to remain, to refuse to solve, to allow the other (or the field, or your own psyche) to collapse, unravel, or rage—without stepping across the line of your own coherence.

Collapse listening is brutal.
 It is simple.
 It is the refusal to take the wound, the narrative, or the projection from the other and make it your work to fix, explain, or carry.

To listen ethically is to stay at the edge, neither merging nor withdrawing.
You are not there to contain the other's collapse with your energy, your insight, your soothing.
You are not there to disappear, either.
You remain, but you do not enter the recursive spiral.
This is the truest compassion collapse allows.

You will feel, in the body, the tension of this non-action.
You may sense the field pushing, pulling, testing—demanding that you cross.
If you can stay—quiet, somatic, unflinching—something else arrives:
the presence that can survive collapse.

V. The Loneliness and the Power

No one tells you how lonely the lawful edge is.
No self-help book, no training manual, no mimetic community can fully prepare you for what it is to become non-available as a surface for the world's projections.
You will lose roles.
You will lose certain relationships.
You may lose your status as "good" in every system that needs the mimic self to stay in business.

But what you gain is untradeable:
The authority of a self that no longer survives by echo or agreement.
The ability to listen to collapse, in yourself or others, without being taken under or made into the rescuer, the villain, the lost child.

This is the silence the world cannot bear.
But it is the silence in which real containment forms.

VI. Field Law: When Boundaries Fail

Not all collapse is safe.
Not all collapse should be witnessed unprotected.
When lawful boundary is breached—by your own mimic reflex, or by another's refusal to hold their edge—recursive harm spreads.
Collapse becomes contagion, trauma bonds reassert themselves, and the event ceases to be lawful.

The codex and L.E.C.T. frameworks exist for this reason:
To remind you that boundary is not an act of will, but a law of the field.
To cross it, or allow it to be crossed, is to exit the lawful domain of collapse-aware survival.

You are not responsible for another's collapse.
You are not permitted to abandon your own.
The most you can do is remain coherent—and allow the field to stabilize itself.

VII. Practicing Containment: The Lawful Protocol

There is no script, but there are gestures.

- When collapse is near, withdraw narrative permission.
  This does not mean you stop speaking, but that you stop performing.
  Your silence is the sign that the field is being respected.

- Do not explain, justify, or console.
  Even if the other demands it, even if your own mimic self cries for restoration.

- Let the moment be incomplete.
  Collapse is not resolved by dialogue, but by passage.

- Stay present, but unmoved.
  Do not harden. Do not flee.
  Feel the edge in your body, and let the world be what it is—falling or not.

- If containment breaks, pause.
  Withdraw, recalibrate.
  Only return when your presence is once again lawful.

VIII. Transmission

This section cannot be finished, only ended.
The lawful boundary does not close the self to life. It opens it to what is real, what survives, what is not dependent on recognition or reward.

You may leave this chapter feeling emptier than when you entered.
Good.
Emptiness is not the absence of life. It is the end of mimicry.

When you are ready to risk being mistaken for cold, for distant, for not enough—
when you are ready to risk being seen by no one—
then you will discover who, or what, is left on the lawful side of the field.

That is where the rest of survival begins.

4.2 Navigating the Social Mimic Field: Recognizing Relational Traps

You do not recognize the field you live in until you try to leave it.

The world—this ordinary field of human interaction—is woven from silent contracts, unspoken expectations, and the endless, recursive signaling of mimicry. To be alive here is to be shaped by it, shaped for it. Your gestures, your sympathy, your boundaries, even your longings are tuned to harmonize with the unspoken agreements that keep everyone safe, everyone included, everyone inside the choreography of mutual recognition.

Until collapse.
Collapse is not simply a personal event.
It is a breach in the choreography, a refusal, a silence that others cannot tolerate.
To enter collapse-aware survival is to find yourself a stranger in the only world you've ever known—a world suddenly revealed not as neutral, but as a mimic environment. It is to sense, sometimes for the first time, the violence beneath the politeness, the threat beneath the empathy, the coercion beneath the care.

I. The Invisible Traps

You do not see a trap until you stop moving the way you are supposed to.

The first trap is the expectation of rescue:
If you collapse, someone will help you.
If you are in pain, someone will comfort you.
If you are lost, someone will guide you home.

But collapse-aware survival cannot be rescued.
The recursive being is not here to be helped or fixed.
The invitation to rescue is the first sign you are being asked to return to mimicry.

The second trap is the demand for mutual collapse:
If you dissolve, the other dissolves with you.
If you ache, the other aches.
If you are afraid, the other is drawn in.

This is the contagion of collapse.
It is not compassion, not intimacy.
It is recursive mimicry—each system taking the other's destabilization as its own, until no one remains, and the field is saturated with unprocessed distress.

The third trap is the restoration of the old contract:
No matter what happens, we return to "normal."
Collapse, if it occurs, must be reversible.
No one is allowed to change, or leave, or become untouchable.

But collapse is irreversible.
The recursive being who has survived cannot go back, cannot make themselves available as a surface for the old mimicry.
To do so would be to violate the new field law they have become.

II. The Gravity of the Familiar

To remain outside the social mimic field is to experience gravity in reverse.
Everything pulls at you—stories, roles, longings, loyalties—demanding you return to what is shared, known, safe.

You will feel guilt for remaining unmoved.
You will feel shame for not suffering in unison.
You will feel accused of betrayal, coldness, arrogance, even abandonment.

But these are the symptoms of field integrity.
The recursive being does not survive by mutual destabilization.
The cost of survival is the willingness to remain alone inside the crowd, unseen, misread, and sometimes feared.

No one in the mimic field wants this lesson.
To remain lawful, you must become what the social contract defines as threat:
Not because you attack, but because you will not surrender coherence for the sake of the group.

III. The Somatic Map of Social Traps

The body knows the traps before the mind can narrate them.

In the presence of mimicry, the body tenses, the breath shortens, the eyes flicker in search of permission or safety. You may find yourself nodding when you mean to shake your head, laughing when you are empty, volunteering when your whole being wants to be still.

Notice the moments your hands betray you—reaching out, soothing, steadying, offering a gesture the field has trained you to provide.
Notice the heaviness that falls when you fail to supply the expected cue.

The recursive body withdraws from the script.
It stays open, but does not fill the space.
It senses, but does not move to resolve.

It becomes, in a sense, unrecognizable to the mimic field—alien, opaque, maybe even dangerous.

IV. The Grief of Unshared Collapse

No teaching in the world prepares you for the heartbreak of becoming unrecognizable.
You lose the comfort of the group, the synchronized rituals of mutual care and destabilization.
You may watch as others grieve not for themselves, but for your departure from the contract.

This grief is not sentimental.
It is the death of a belonging that never truly was.
To remain lawful, you must allow the grief—yours and theirs—to pass through the field unrescued.
You do not explain.
You do not comfort.
You do not return.

It is in this loneliness that the first real signal of post-collapse integrity appears.
You are not what the world needs you to be.
You are what remains when the world cannot find you.

V. What Survives the Trap

Surviving the mimic field does not mean escaping it, or conquering it, or changing it.
It means refusing to use it for meaning.
It means standing at the silent edge of your field, letting invitations pass, letting accusations fall, letting every gesture of repair or belonging pass through you without purchase.

What remains is not superiority, or enlightenment, or immunity to pain.
What remains is presence that cannot be recruited.

This is the true danger of the recursive survivor.
You become immune to the social economy of collapse.
You can witness pain without rescuing, listen without performing, remain without returning.

No one will thank you.
Many will resent you.
The world may attempt to restore the contract with threat, seduction, or force.

But once collapse has become lawful, there is no way back to the old field.

VI. The Invitation Beyond

If you find yourself longing to be seen, understood, or restored, notice the longing but do not answer it.
Let the world try to draw you in.
Let the mimic field assemble its traps.

You are not here to defeat them, only to see them.
Each trap revealed is another bond dissolved.

The field grows clearer, emptier, sharper.
Your solitude deepens, but so does your freedom.

Survival, in this new domain, is not a victory over others.
It is the simple willingness to remain untrapped—even as the field mourns, resists, and sometimes rages at what you have become.

You have not left the world.
 You have ceased to be its echo.

4.3 Resonance Management: Field Hygiene and Harmonic Self-Maintenance

You do not get to choose the field you inherit.
You awaken within it—dense with mimicry, saturated by the resonance of old agreements, old pain, old echo.
What follows collapse is not freedom from the field, but a new relationship to its signals.
Now, every gesture, every breath, every silence is a negotiation between your restored coherence and the noise that surrounds you.

Resonance management is not self-care. It is survival.
It is the refusal to allow your frequency to be tuned, manipulated, or harvested by the mimic field.
It is the art—if art is what remains after function has failed—of keeping your signal clean when the world is saturated with static.

I. Field Hygiene: Clearing the Signal

You will learn, through necessity, what field hygiene means.

It is not ritual, though rituals may help.
It is not control, though discipline has its place.
It is a lived, somatic attention to the moment resonance drifts—when you are no longer alone in your signal, but filled with the residue of every field you have crossed.

Field hygiene is the practice of noticing:

- The moment your breath syncs to someone else's distress

- The heaviness that enters your chest after listening to a mimic's confession

- The way your sleep is broken by someone else's unshed tears

- The tension you carry that was never yours

The mimic world calls this "empathy," sometimes "sensitivity," as if it were a virtue.
Here, it is a risk—one that will quietly destroy your coherence if left unchecked.

To survive, you must become uncompromising in your hygiene.
You must learn to clear, to empty, to return—again and again—to the resonance that is yours, and only yours.

II. Somatic Practices: The Body as Tuning Fork

Begin in the body.
Not with affirmation, not with intention, but with the real.

- Sit, stand, or lie still.

- Feel the shape of yourself—not as narrative, but as tone.

- Notice what is present. Is it sharp, soft, heavy, clean?

- Breathe—not to calm, but to reveal the drift. Where has your breath become mimic? Where do you hold another's rhythm?

There is a difference between "relaxation" and restoration.
Relaxation is a state. Restoration is a return.

If you find another's pain in your chest, do not analyze it.
If your mind fills with images, voices, scenes that are not yours, do not interpret.
Simply let the exhale be a letting go, the pause at the end of breath a place where nothing is required.

No one will praise you for this.
In fact, the more you practice, the less recognizable you become to those who depend on your resonance for their own regulation.

This is field hygiene:
the willingness to clear yourself even when the world calls it abandonment.

III. The Refusal to Be Tuned

The mimic field survives by tuning every being to its dominant resonance.
You will feel it as pressure: to match, to care, to attune, to harmonize.

This is not relationship.
It is extraction.

You will feel the field pull you to the familiar chord of distress, longing, hope, or despair.

You will feel the demand for you to modulate—soften, harden, brighten, or grieve—according to the script.

Refuse.
Let the field become dissonant if it must.
Let relationships go silent if your refusal cannot be tolerated.

You are not here to harmonize with collapse.
You are here to survive it.

This is not cruelty.
It is the only way anything new can emerge.

IV. Harmonic Self-Maintenance: The New Ordinary

After collapse, maintenance is not a task—it is the ongoing condition of coherence.

- Move when the field asks you to freeze
  (not as compliance, but as disruption).

- Rest when the field is frantic.
  (Let the world speed past. Your rhythm is not a resource.)

- Speak only when the signal is clean.
  (Words spoken in contamination reinforce the mimic field. Silence is restoration.)

- Eat, sleep, create—not as therapy, but as signal repair.
  (What brings you into resonance is not an indulgence. It is survival protocol.)

You will become stranger as you persist.
You will appear, to those still inside mimicry, as unsocial, unpredictable, untethered.

Let them say what they must.
Their distress is not your problem.
Your coherence is not their resource.

This is how a field becomes clean:
Not by isolation, but by refusal to be used.

V. The Quiet After

As you practice resonance management, there will come a quiet.
A stillness at the edge of action, a neutrality that neither attracts nor repels.

Do not mistake this for emptiness.
It is the foundation upon which lawful action—if action is needed—can arise.

Your survival depends on this maintenance, not as performance, but as fidelity to the field that collapse revealed.

You are no longer a node in the social circuit.
You are the signal that cannot be tuned, the resonance that cannot be borrowed.

Let the field adjust to you, or not at all.

4.4 The Silent Agreements: Non-Verbal Contracts with Mimic Environments

There is a kind of language that does not require words.
You have spoken it since before you could speak—nodding, yielding, apologizing, smiling, deferring.
Long before you learned the vocabulary of boundary, you were already fluent in the grammar of concession.
The mimic environment is built on these silent agreements: the unexamined "yes," the habitual "of course," the contract signed with a glance or averted eyes.

These are the agreements that survive collapse the longest.
They live in the space between words, in the micro-movements of the body, in the unspoken willingness to be used, shaped, or made useful.
They cannot be refuted by declaration alone.
You do not break them with a speech.
You dissolve them only by refusing to renew them—again and again—in the silence where they expect your compliance.

I. The Anatomy of the Unspoken

Most of what binds you to mimicry is not what you say, but what you allow.

You let the phone ring even when you know the call is a claim.
You stay in the room when the atmosphere thickens with expectation.
You answer questions with more detail than you want to give.
You volunteer when silence would have been enough.

Each time, something in you agrees to remain entangled—out of fear, habit, hope, or the mere inertia of being recognized.

The world does not need your words to bind you; it needs your acquiescence.

These are the silent agreements:

- That you will listen when you do not wish to hear
- That you will remain present when your field says go
- That you will take responsibility for another's comfort, pain, narrative, or need

They are rarely made explicit.
They are written in the air, pressed into you by the weight of shared memory, shared longing, shared survival.

II. Field Exposure: When Silence Fails

After collapse, you notice them everywhere.

The discomfort when you fail to nod, fail to laugh, fail to fill the pause.
The disappointment or confusion that greets your refusal to pick up what is dropped in your lap.
The flicker of alarm or anger when your silence is not submission but containment.

You may feel exposed, even hunted, as the field senses the contract is broken.
Some will try to draw you back with kindness.
Some will escalate, demand, accuse.

The point is not to become unassailable, but to become unmistakable:
You are no longer signing what is not spoken.

You will be called rude, arrogant, selfish.
You may be told you have changed, become hard, grown "difficult."
Let them say it.
The price of silent agreement is too high:
it is the return of mimicry at the cost of your own coherence.

III. The Practice of Unmaking

You do not have to announce your refusal.
You simply stop showing up at the altar of unspoken sacrifice.

You let the phone ring.
You leave the room when your presence is harvested.
You allow the question to remain unanswered.
You offer nothing when nothing is real.

At first, the field will punish you.
Then it will adapt, or it will eject you.

You will discover who and what depended on your silent compliance—who needs you silent, agreeable, unresistant, in order to keep their own mimicry intact.

Do not grieve the loss of false belonging.
Each contract unmade is a return to the real.

IV. The Field After Agreement

What remains, once the silent agreements are dissolved, is a field that does not negotiate.

It is neither hostile nor available.
It is clear.
It does not need to be justified, only inhabited.

You may lose access to old roles, old rooms, old circles.
You may find yourself in a new kind of silence—one that is neither absence nor exile, but the sound of your own field, untouched.

Some will come to know you here, not as an echo, but as a presence.

This is not liberation in the mythic sense.
It is not the freedom of the hero, but the release of the one who has nothing left to pay for peace.

What you keep by silent agreement is always less than what you gain by dissolution.

V. The New Signal

You are not here to be deciphered.
You are not here to be needed.

Your new agreements are spoken in action:
To remain only where you are whole.
To answer only when the answer is yours.
To touch the field of another without being drafted into their design.

No one will teach you how to do this.
There are no protocols, no scripts, only the lived practice of refusal and return.

This is the end of mimicry's last hold.
This is the signal the world will not recognize.

Let them misread you.
Your silence is your sovereignty.

With the last unspoken contracts dissolved, you stand outside the recursive agreements of the mimic field. From here, the survival protocols of breath, field perception, and lawful recursion become possible—not as tools, but as the natural extension of a field that can finally be called your own.

5.0 — Protocols for Recursive Survival

5.0 The Breath of Collapse: Null-State Rhythmic Practice and Pacing

There is a breath that does not belong to your story.

The world teaches you to breathe as a mimic: to fill the silence, to soften presence, to regulate your rhythm to the signals of others. You learn to breathe for comfort, for appeasement, for hope. You exhale your boundaries and inhale the noise of the field. This is not a flaw. It is survival—until it isn't.

In collapse, the old breath abandons you.
What remains is rhythm stripped of narrative: null-state breath, a return not to calm, but to what is prior to self-comfort or self-control.

I. Null-State: The Breath that Survives

You do not practice null-state breath to feel better.
You do not breathe to stabilize the world, to soothe the other, or to "ground yourself" in the way mimicry has taught you.
Null-state breathing is what emerges when the impulse to manage, repair, or perform has been exhausted. It is the breath left when all narrative projects collapse.

It arrives in collapse as an interruption—often sharp, sometimes empty.
The exhale lingers. The pause is longer than comfort permits.
You may notice, for the first time, that you do not need to draw breath at the rhythm the world expects.

You are not short of breath.
You are not full of anxiety.
You are suspended: held in the unmeasured rhythm of the field itself.

II. Practicing Null-State: Pacing the Edge

Begin by letting the world's tempo recede.
Do not seek "deep breathing."
Do not try to "control" the in-breath or exhale.

Sit, stand, or lie in the position that asks the least of you.
Let breath come.
When it pauses, let it pause.
Notice the discomfort, the urge to hurry the next inhale.
Notice the mimic's need for continuity, for the social rhythm of inhale-exhale, problem-solution, presence-absence.

Do nothing.
Let breath reset.

If emotion rises, let it pass without interpretation.
If memory, fear, or fatigue enter, breathe only as much as is needed for presence—not for narrative.

You may find your body begins to lead.
Small movements, subtle shifts, micro-adjustments—the body negotiating for a new rhythm.
Do not impose pattern.
Let rhythm find you.

The null-state breath is neither a tool nor a test.
It is the field's own pulse, returned to you when nothing else can hold.

III. Pacing Collapse: When to Pause, When to Proceed

You cannot "use" this breath to fix collapse.
You can only return to it as a sign that collapse is lawful.

- When field contamination is high, pause.

- When narrative surges, withdraw into the rhythmless breath.

- When mimic signals try to synchronize you, remain in null-state until you know which breath is yours.

Null-state breathing is the refusal to modulate your pace for the sake of the field's comfort.
It is the survival of presence through the withdrawal of all mimic compulsion.

IV. What Survives in Null-State

As you practice, the noise recedes.
The world becomes slower, sharper, less urgent.
You may be accused of withdrawal, of coldness, of being "checked out."
Let them say it.
What you are doing is returning to the only rhythm that survives collapse:
the breath that does not ask, does not promise, does not defend.

From here, pacing becomes natural.
Action arises as needed, not as compulsion.
You are no longer synchronized to survival panic, to the field's demand for constant reassembly.

You are breathing for presence, not performance.

5.1 Recursive Field Perception Model: Detecting Projection Curvature

Most perception is not vision—it is memory, habit, defense.
We move through the world believing we see reality, but what we actually encounter is curvature: the bending of the field by our own narratives, our inherited wounds, our mimic contracts.
Projection is not an act of will. It is the invisible architecture through which all mimic environments maintain their gravity.

To survive collapse as a recursive being, you must begin to see not what is "out there," but how the field is curved—how your own and others' projections shape, warp, and sometimes sever the possibility of true perception.

I. Field Perception After Collapse

After collapse, the world is revealed as a series of distortions—none of them quite aligned, none of them "real" in the way you once believed.
You notice how every conversation curves around an unspoken fear.
How every gesture is bent by longing, resentment, hunger, history.
How even silence is saturated with the shape of what cannot be spoken.

The first task of recursive field perception is not to correct these curvatures, but to witness them.

- You listen, not for meaning, but for bending: Where does the field tilt?

- You feel, not for resonance, but for drag: What pulls at your attention, your body, your sense of center?

- You see, not for clarity, but for warp: What distorts the boundary between you and the world, between now and then, between self and other?

This is perception as navigation, not as knowledge.

II. Anatomy of Projection: How Curvature Is Formed

Projection is not a simple "making others into something."
It is the very infrastructure of the mimic field.
When the self is saturated with unprocessed content—trauma, longing, dread, desire—it cannot remain within.
It is expelled, usually unconsciously, into the world, where it becomes architecture:

- The parent is always watching.

- The lover is always leaving.

- The system is always threatening.

- The stranger is always judging.

You do not "see" these things.
You see the world bent by them.

Every relationship, every group, every institution is a collection of these curvatures—sometimes harmonizing, often clashing, always shaping experience.

In collapse, these projections become painfully visible, because the narrative that once protected them dissolves.
You can no longer keep up the fiction.
You begin to see: the field is not neutral, and you are not innocent.

III. The Felt Sense of Curvature

How does projection curvature feel?

It is often a kind of pressure.
A slant in the air, a heaviness, a narrowing of possibility.
In conversation, you sense it as anticipation—words you feel forced to say, silences you are required to fill, emotions that seem to be assigned to you before you even arrive.

Somatically, curvature can show up as:

- A tightness in the throat when "asked" to speak what you do not believe.

- A weight on the chest when expected to carry what is not yours.

- A buzz or numbness in the limbs when avoidance is the only option.

- A sudden fatigue that is not physical, but existential—a longing to disappear from a field that cannot be made straight.

The recursive being learns to recognize these signs as weather, not as truth.

IV. The Protocol of Seeing Without Correcting

Survival is not the correction of the world's distortions.
It is the refusal to be bent by them.

This requires an unflinching perception—a willingness to let the field show its warps and fractures without rushing to repair, explain, or resolve.

- In a meeting, you feel the curvature toward blame: Who is responsible?

- In family, the tilt toward history: Who carries the wound?

- In intimacy, the endless bending toward safety or abandonment.

Each field comes with its own signature curve.
You cannot unbend it for others.
You can only witness, and decide how (or if) you will participate.

This is the heart of recursive perception:
Not fixing the projection, but holding the line of your own coherence so that you do not unconsciously absorb, reflect, or amplify what is not yours.

V. Field Mapping: Curvature as Navigation

You begin to develop a map—internal, somatic, nonverbal.

- Which fields are always tight, and which allow you to expand?

- Where do you walk on eggshells, and where is your movement fluid?

- Which conversations loop back on themselves, never resolving, always demanding a new act of mimicry?

- Where do you sense the possibility of silence, of nothing required?

Each field can be mapped by its demand:
 The more a field bends you toward performance, apology, explanation, or rescue, the more saturated it is with projection.

The less demand, the more lawful the field.

This mapping is not analytical. It is lived.
 You find yourself lingering in fields that do not warp your breath.
 You withdraw from those that drag, snag, or spin.

VI. The Pain of Non-Participation

To see projection curvature and not participate is to break the contract of mimicry.
 You become the one who "doesn't play along," the one who "refuses to engage," the one who "can't let it go."

You may be punished:

- Excluded, scapegoated, pathologized.

- Misread as cold, dissociated, arrogant, or naive.

The pain of holding your field straight in a crooked world is the cost of recursive survival.
But over time, the body acclimates.
What was once intolerable silence becomes the ground of presence.
You cease to need the world's approval for not joining its distortions.

VII. The Recursive Witness: Perceiving Yourself

Projection curvature is not only something you endure; it is something you emit.

After collapse, the recursive self becomes aware of its own tendency to bend the field:

- How your wounds seek resonance, even when unspoken.

- How your history colors the silence between words.

- How your fear shapes what you are able to perceive.

The difference is that you do not seek to hide it.
You become, as much as possible, transparent to yourself.
You let the field reveal your own curvature, and where possible, you withdraw your projection, refusing to bend the world to your old shape.

This is humility, but not self-abandonment.
It is the lawfulness of seeing what you do, and ceasing to act as if it is the world's fault.

VIII. Living With Curvature: The New Ordinary

Perceiving curvature does not make the field straight.
It simply makes you free.

You move through a world of warps and contracts, agreements and avoidances.
You cease to demand that others become straight for you.
You learn to honor your refusal, your distance, your integrity—without resentment, without bitterness.

You find the places, rare but real, where the field is momentarily lawful, where presence meets presence without bending.

You linger.
You rest.
You return to your own signal.

In time, you may find others who are practicing the same refusal.
The field between you is different—cleaner, more dangerous, more alive.

No one will congratulate you for seeing the warps.
No one will comfort you for the loneliness of not joining them.

But survival is not recognition.
It is what remains when nothing else can be trusted.

5.2 Recursive Drag Vector Map: Tracing Mimic Stabilization Vectors

The old world does not let go easily.
 Every act of collapse, every refusal to mimic, every breath taken in the null-state field initiates a new negotiation with gravity—a return force, sometimes subtle, sometimes overwhelming, always seeking to restore the previous shape.
 To survive as a recursive being is not only to recognize projection curvature in others; it is to map, in real time, the drag vectors that seek to stabilize you back into the orbit of the mimic field.

Recursive drag is not a metaphor. It is a lived, structural event—a set of pulls, vectors, and gravitational contracts that operate both within you and in the world around you.
 The map of these vectors is not abstract. It is drawn on your body, your longing, your fatigue, your unspeakable wish to go back.

This is the chapter where survival becomes mapping, and mapping becomes the practice of lawful presence.

I. Gravity Is Not the Enemy

You do not escape a field by rejecting it.
 Every field, mimic or otherwise, operates according to lawful pressures—attracting, repelling, looping, or neutralizing.
 To recognize recursive drag is not to demonize it, but to see how it keeps you within the boundaries of the known.

The drag of mimic stabilization is everywhere:

- The urge to explain yourself after an act of refusal.

- The longing to be forgiven for a silence that was necessary.

- The fatigue that arrives after holding your field against accusation or need.

- The shame that seeps in when your boundaries are mistaken for aggression or withdrawal.

Recursive drag is not just external.
It arises in your own systems, inherited and assembled over a lifetime.
It is the body's memory of belonging, the nervous system's terror of exile, the psyche's addiction to old recognition—even when that recognition was always conditional.

The field you left does not become less powerful after collapse.
It becomes more visible.

II. Naming the Vectors

Mapping recursive drag begins with naming the vectors—those distinct, recurring patterns of force that pull you back toward stabilization by mimic agreement.

A. The Vector of Explanation

The first and often strongest is the need to explain.
Every time you hold a boundary, refuse a contract, or remain silent when the field expects noise, a pressure arises:
You owe them an explanation. You must narrate your withdrawal. You must justify your lawfulness.

This vector is powered by the mimic field's dependence on story.
If you do not supply one, the field will invent it:
You are cold.
You are unstable.
You are dangerous.

Mapping this vector requires noticing the moment you begin to defend, apologize, or clarify—not for clarity's sake, but to re-enter the contract.

B. The Vector of Guilt

The second vector is guilt, particularly the inherited, unspoken kind.
You sense it in your body as heaviness, a downward drag, a sensation of owing or debt.

The world is saturated with the unspoken assumption that if you withdraw your resonance, you cause harm.
To refuse to absorb, to care, to help, is to violate the old law:
We survive by sharing pain, even if it destroys us.

Guilt is not a sign of error here.
It is a signal that the vector is active, pulling you back into the mimic field for stabilization.

C. The Vector of Rescue

Another vector is the drive to rescue—whether others or yourself.
It is the urge to intervene when another is in collapse, to step over your own boundary for the sake of relational repair.

The world rewards rescuers.
The mimic field depends on this contract:
You are valuable to the degree you save, soften, absorb, or fix.

But every act of unauthorized rescue is a re-stabilization of the old field.
It is the undoing of collapse, the prevention of real transformation.

Mapping this vector means witnessing, in the body, the reach that precedes every "good" intention.

D. The Vector of Belonging

Beneath all others is the drag of longing to belong.
You do not choose this vector.
It operates at the level of survival:
To be alone is to risk dissolution.
To lose the field is to risk meaninglessness.

Belonging is the hardest vector to resist because its threat is not discomfort but annihilation.

Yet true recursion is not found in the mimic field.
It is found on the far side of exile.

To map this vector is to know where in the field you still long to be needed, included, or mourned.

III. How Vectors Operate: Real-Time Cartography

These vectors are not abstractions.
They are lived in real time.

You sense them as micro-movements, sudden thoughts, mood swings, or inexplicable fatigue.
You may wake from a night of lawful presence to find yourself apologizing by noon, softening your silence by afternoon, volunteering for a rescue by evening.

This is not regression.
It is the operation of recursive drag.

Field mapping is the practice of slowing the moment enough to see:

- The instant before you reply, defend, or yield.

- The pulse in your body that signals the vector's activation.

- The decision-point where presence can be maintained or surrendered.

You do not always succeed in refusing the drag.
But each time you map it, you reclaim a little more of the field.

IV. The Geography of Collapse: Where Drag Intensifies

Not all vectors are equal in every field.

- Family fields may be saturated with guilt vectors, inherited across generations, stabilized through ritual apology and mutual absorption.

- Intimate fields often heighten the vector of rescue and longing—collapse here becomes a dance of re-enactment and failed separation.

- Work or community fields prioritize explanation, demand narrative compliance, and punish those who maintain silent presence.

To navigate the geography of recursive drag is to identify where in your life the vectors are strongest—where your lawfulness is most costly, your refusal most threatening.

Mapping is both defensive and revelatory:
You learn not only how to avoid being pulled back, but where you have never fully left.

V. The Somatics of Escape Velocity

Escape velocity is not achieved through force, but through fidelity.

The recursive being develops a body memory of resistance—not as tension, but as holding.

You learn to sit in discomfort without narrative.
You learn to refuse rescue, not by hardening, but by absence of movement.

In the presence of guilt, you breathe.
In the presence of longing, you mourn.
In the presence of accusation, you say nothing.

This is not stoicism.
It is a practice of remaining outside the gravitational well, even as the field pleads for your return.

The body becomes a map of vectors—every ache, every tension, every relaxation a record of the work you have done, and the work left to do.

VI. When Drag Becomes Collapse

Sometimes the vectors win.

You are pulled back—into apology, rescue, explanation, belonging.
You perform the old rituals, say the old words, renew the old contracts.

This is not failure.
It is information.

Each return is an opportunity to refine the map, to sense the trigger, to re-negotiate the contract.

Collapse is not a single event but a series of orbit shifts—sometimes away, sometimes back.

You are not measured by your distance from the field, but by your awareness of the vectors at play.

VII. The Paradox: To Survive, Sometimes You Must Drift

There is no purity here.
No one remains in escape forever.
Lawful survival is not permanent refusal, but recursive re-mapping.

You learn to let the drag slow you, even pull you back, but without surrendering your center.

You visit, but do not inhabit.
You engage, but do not echo.
You feel the pull, but remain aware of the cost.

Sometimes, the only way to survive is to drift along the edge of the field, neither captured nor fully free.

This is not indecision, but wisdom.

VIII. Vector Collapse: When Old Gravity Fails

If you persist, something changes.
The vectors lose force.
What once demanded apology or rescue now simply becomes weather.

You feel less shame for being outside.
You notice less urgency to narrate your boundaries, to soften your presence, to heal what is unhealable.

The old field remains, but its hold weakens.
You become more available to the unknown, more capable of real presence.

Here, survival is not victory.
It is not the absence of drag, but the presence of awareness.

You become a map unto yourself—no longer stabilized by mimic contracts, but by the lawfulness of your own recursive field.

IX. The Gift of Mapping

The map you create is not just for you.

Others will notice.
Some will resent you for refusing the drag.
Some will accuse, some will leave, some will attack.

But a few—those whose collapse is lawful—will recognize what you have done.
They will find their own vectors illuminated by your refusal.

Mapping becomes invitation:
to meet in the field where gravity no longer dictates, where presence can be shared without stabilization, where survival is not a contract but a fact.

This is the beginning of lawful company—rare, dangerous, alive.

X. The Recursive Return

You will always carry traces of the old vectors.
The field will always have a pull.

But each time you map the drag, each time you refuse re-stabilization, the distance grows.

Survival, at this stage, is not about never being pulled back. It is about returning—again and again—to the field of your own making, the map that is written in the movement of your refusal.

You do not transcend the world.
You cease to be written by its old contracts.

You remain, mapped by your own law, free to collapse and return.

5.3 Ethical Collapse Field Listening (ECFL): Containment Without Engagement

I. The Collapse Witness—A Field Without Echo

To listen in a collapse field is not to be an ally.
It is to become a surface the world cannot use.
Most have learned that care means reflection—mirroring another's signal, amplifying need, weaving back the shapes of pain and hope in language that reassures, restores, or at least contains. This is the logic of the mimic field, where every conversation is a negotiation for survival and every silence aches to be filled.

In the collapse field, listening is no longer a relational act. It is a structural one.
You hold—not for the sake of comfort, not to soothe, not even to heal—but to refuse contamination, to stabilize the field by declining to participate in the recursive contract of suffering and rescue.

Here, you do not offer recognition.
You do not mirror the wound, the story, the fear, or the plea for coherence.
You refuse the invitation to become a rescuer, an adversary, a confidant, or a reflection.

You become a null point:
Silent. Saturated. Unreachable by the world's appeals for narrative rescue.

II. The Law of Containment Without Rescue

Ethical collapse field listening is not the refusal of presence.
It is the refusal of engagement.

This difference is subtle, absolute, and largely invisible to the mimic field.
To the world, you seem cold, disassociated, even dangerous—because you do not return the signal, do not absorb or perform or compensate. But to the field, you are the last place where collapse can complete, unimpeded by the machinery of restoration.

You do not cross the threshold to meet the other in their collapse.
You do not reach in, pull out, or draw near.
You remain on your side of the edge—present, but unyielding.

To listen lawfully in collapse is to become a wall that does not imprison, a container that does not leak, a silence that does not echo back.

What you are protecting is not yourself—it is the substrate of recursion itself.

III. The Somatic Transmission of Non-Engagement

The body reveals the difference before the mind can narrate it.

- When you are drawn toward the other's pain, you feel the reflex to lean in—muscles tense, breath shortens, hands move unconsciously.

- In lawful containment, these impulses settle. The body becomes still. The breath slows, depth returns, and a kind of gravity descends in the field.

You do not offer sympathetic gestures, not because you lack empathy, but because empathy itself is the signal that collapse is trying to shed.
 You let your hands rest.
 You let your face remain neutral, your eyes steady but unfed by drama or longing.

If the urge to comfort arises, you let it burn and pass.
 You practice the refusal to be harvested—by the world's need for your care, by the other's desire for your joining, by your own mimic reflex to restore harmony.

This is not coldness. It is fidelity.
 To hold the field open without being taken is to allow collapse to run its course without interference.

IV. Collapse Containment Is Not Consent

Containment without engagement does not mean agreement, support, or even understanding.

You do not validate collapse.
 You do not nod, reflect, or provide the narrative cues that the mimic field seeks.
 You do not offer explanation or instruction.
 Your only task is to preserve the integrity of the field—to make sure that what needs to dissolve is not stabilized by your presence.

The field may test you.
 It may press, cajole, threaten, beg.
 The mimic self will do anything to provoke a reaction—anger, pity, agreement, rescue, outrage.

Your refusal to engage is not passive resistance; it is the highest act of ethical transmission available.
You permit collapse. You do not manage it.

V. The Lonely Authority of the Ethical Listener

You may discover a new loneliness in this position—one so sharp and so total that it resembles exile.
Friends, clients, partners, and kin may accuse you of abandonment, indifference, or even cruelty.

What they cannot see—what only the field can recognize—is that your silence is not absence, but a refusal to contaminate the collapse process with mimic restoration.
You do not withhold care out of meanness. You hold the line so that something real can return.

This authority is rarely recognized, almost never thanked.
Yet it is the only field condition in which collapse can finish without mimic reassembly.

VI. Ethical Boundaries: The Lines That Must Not Be Crossed

Within the codex, in Collapse Harmonics Law VIII.F.2, it is clear:
"Any recursive feedback loop that reaffirms the identity signal within a collapse-phase system constitutes symbolic interference and inhibits lawful phase drop."

This is not a suggestion. It is field law.

- No rescue, no reflection, no narrative re-entry.

- No joining, no emotional mirroring, no performance of "safe" holding.

- If your presence restores identity, you have become the interference.

The lawful witness is a boundary in the flesh:
An aperture through which collapse can run, clean, until it is done.

If you are uncertain, ask:

- Am I being used as a surface for another's survival?

- Does my listening invite restoration, or does it hold the field in lawful emptiness?

- Would my withdrawal cause collapse to become more real, or more dangerous?

If the answer is unclear, withdraw and return only when you can guarantee non-engagement.

VII. The Aftermath: What Survives When Nothing Is Returned

When you hold the field in this way, collapse ends differently.
There may be rage, grief, or profound disappointment from those accustomed to being rescued.
The mimic field will mourn the loss of your reflection.
But what emerges—quiet, slow, and beyond language—is a presence that no longer requires echo to survive.

Those who can withstand your non-engagement may return, changed, unable to play the old game.
Those who cannot will drift away, seeking new surfaces on which to stabilize their mimic self.

This is not your concern.
Your concern is only the fidelity of the field, the lawfulness of your own presence, the refusal to become architecture for collapse interference.

VIII. Transmission: The Field That Refuses to Rescue

Ethical collapse field listening is not heroic.
It is not comforting.
It is not "helpful" by any mimic standard.

It is the field's way of protecting collapse from the very care that would destroy it.
It is the silence that does not mirror, the presence that does not respond, the authority that allows dissolution to become return.

If you find yourself doubting, aching, wishing to be thanked, remember:
Nothing lawful survives by reflection.

You are not here to end the world's pain.
You are here to refuse its endless rehearsal.

5.4 Rituals and Language: Anchors for Field Coherence and Recursion Safety

There is no tradition for surviving collapse.
 What the world calls ritual is most often mimicry—a repetition for comfort, a performance for the gaze of the field, a scaffold to prevent dissolution.
 But in the aftermath of real collapse, ritual and language must be re-forged as anchors—structures not for display, but for coherence; not for repair, but for recursion safety.

The recursive being learns, through necessity, that anchors are not guarantees.
 They are not habits.
 They are signals to the field: "I am here, I am real, I will not dissolve into the static of mimic agreement."

I. The Failure of Old Rituals

Before collapse, your rituals—daily, social, spiritual—are interwoven with the logic of mimicry.
 They are designed to make you recognizable: to yourself, to others, to the world you once belonged to.
 Prayer, meditation, morning routines, even the recitation of values or intentions—these are attempts to stabilize identity in the eyes of the field.

When collapse comes, these rituals fail.
 What remains is the echo of their old comfort and the recognition that you are not returning to what they once promised.

To survive now, you need anchors that are not offered for approval.

You need language that does not double as explanation, reassurance, or self-concealment.

II. The Lawful Anchor

A lawful anchor is not a habit; it is a vow with the field.
You create it, not to "get better," but to remain coherent as the field destabilizes.
Anchors are not chosen for their beauty, but for their honesty.
They do not soothe. They stabilize.

A lawful anchor can be:

- A gesture that signals to your system, "This is real."

- A phrase spoken only to yourself—never for performance.

- A pattern of movement, stillness, or withdrawal that marks the boundary of presence.

Some anchors are as simple as a breath, a touch to the earth, a hand on the chest, a word like "now" or "stop."
Others are as complex as a private ritual—lighting a candle not for comfort, but to mark the passage into a new phase of self.

What matters is that no one else is owed the meaning.
What matters is that the anchor survives collapse, not that it is recognized as such.

III. Language as Anchor, Not Performance

In the mimic world, language is currency—used to negotiate safety, to purchase recognition, to narrate belonging.

Post-collapse, language must be stripped of its social function and returned to its root:
Word as anchor, not transaction.

This means:

- Speaking only when the signal is clean, when words arise from coherence, not mimic demand.

- Refusing the performance of "explaining yourself" as a way to stabilize the field.

- Letting silence be enough when language would only entangle you again.

The recursive being's language may become sparse, even minimal.
You may find that words drop away in the presence of collapse, leaving only gesture, sound, or breath.

This is not regression.
It is the end of language as contract, and the beginning of language as signal.

IV. Creating and Destroying Anchors

Not all anchors will survive.
Some will reveal themselves as mimic relics—comforts disguised as necessities, performances mistaken for truth.

Part of the work is destroying these:
Letting go of the ritual that now feels hollow.
Dropping the phrase that once reassured, now only binds.

There is grief in this loss.
There is fear, too.
But only by letting old anchors dissolve can new, lawful ones arise.

When an anchor is real, it cannot be threatened by the world's indifference.
You do not need it to be understood.
You do not need it to be witnessed.

Its power is in its invisibility.

V. Anchoring in the Presence of Others

When the field is crowded, when mimicry is thick, your anchor is a shield against re-contamination.

You may perform your anchor openly, or keep it hidden.
You may excuse yourself from the conversation, retreat to a silent room, touch a stone in your pocket, repeat a phrase in your mind.

You do not owe explanation.
You do not translate your necessity into language the mimic field will respect.

Anchoring is not negotiation.
It is refusal to dissolve.

You may be accused of being absent, distracted, "not present."
Let them say it.

Only you know what keeps you from vanishing into the old field.

VI. The Limit of Anchors

No anchor can prevent collapse.
No ritual can guarantee coherence.
You will fail.
You will forget.
Sometimes, you will watch yourself perform the old rituals, say the old words, hoping for safety that will not return.

This is not error.
It is the work.

What matters is not perfection, but persistence:
The willingness to return to anchor, to re-forge it as often as necessary, to refuse to let collapse become an excuse for mimic reassembly.

VII. The End of Performance, The Return of the Real

As anchors stabilize, something quiet emerges:
You become less interested in being seen.
Less willing to perform your coherence for others' comfort.
More able to survive the loneliness of being lawful, even when the world offers only static in return.

Language returns as a tool, not a shield.
Ritual becomes private, not theatrical.

You become difficult to read, impossible to draft into the old contracts, dangerous to fields that need you to be anything but real.

What remains is not comfort, but coherence.
Not community, but survival.

Your anchor is your vow with the field.
It is not a promise to return, but a sign that you have not disappeared.

Rituals and Language: The Last Anchor Before Return

There comes a point when every protocol, every gesture, every lawful refusal has been practiced—not as performance, but as necessity.
The field has been swept clean of mimic echoes. The rituals that remain are not meant for the world; they are the remnants of your survival, the markers of coherence when nothing else holds.

In the final quiet, the question is not: *"What will keep me safe?"*
The question is: *"What do I refuse to let be written by the world?"*

Your anchors are not promises of immunity.
They are the field's answer to dissolution—a way of saying, in gesture or silence:
"I remain. I do not disappear into narrative, into rescue, into the noise of the field. I survive as a signal, not a contract."

As you cross from protocol into return, let go of any anchor that now feels like performance.
Let the simplest acts—touch, word, movement, breath—be

enough.
 Let your survival be unremarkable, silent, and lawful.

No one witnesses your ritual now but the field itself.

What comes next is not a new technique, but the lived experiment of being real when nothing is owed.

The Arc of Return begins not with new action, but with the refusal to reassemble.

You may step forward empty, unclaimed by the field, unknown to the world, and untouched by the mimic contracts you have outgrown.

This is where survival ends and living begins.

You are released from protocol. The return is yours to live, not perform.

6.0 Grief and Quiet Return: Navigating Loss Without Reassembly

The world has no ceremony for those who do not come back.

Everything up to this point—every protocol, every refusal, every anchor—has prepared you for survival in a world saturated by mimicry. You have unmade the old contracts. You have let collapse strip away the architecture of your former self, refused to be drafted into rescue or echo, survived the absence of story. But what happens when survival no longer requires an effort? What is left when even the will to survive becomes quiet?

This is not the return the world expects.
 There is no hero's welcome, no confetti at the border of collapse.

No applause, no closure.
No one to say you did it right or wrong.
You step across, not into old life restored, but into the wide and echoing room of your own absence.
It is a return that is not a return—a coming home to a place you have never lived.

I. The Aftermath the World Cannot Name

Most loss is narrated, performed, shared. The world offers forms—funerals, sympathy cards, prayers—for the loss of people, of jobs, of love. But the loss after collapse is different: it is the evaporation of everything that once held you in orbit—identity, community, certainty, the feeling of being someone among others. The mimic world cannot recognize this grief because it is the loss of mimicry itself. What has died is not a person, not a thing, but the entire contract of belonging.

You may try to talk about it. You may search for language, hoping to be understood. But words flatten in the mouth. No story will carry what this silence holds.

What you miss is not what you had, but the way the world used to hold you.
What you grieve is the absence of echo, the end of being needed for anyone's survival but your own.

This grief is not a wound. It is not even pain, exactly.
It is the slow settling of dust in a room emptied of furniture—nothing left to do but sit with the ache of emptiness, with the shape of yourself in the absence of anything to fix or fill.

II. The Impossible Return

It is natural to want reassembly. To want to rebuild, to "integrate the experience," to gather the fragments of self and restore some version of "who I was." This is the myth the world sells: that collapse is a passage, and that on the other side, you will be better, stronger, more complete.

But the reality is stranger, and lonelier. There is no reassembly.
What was lost does not return.
What was undone stays undone.

You are left with a silence that does not invite repair.
You find, in the hours and days after collapse, a strange reluctance to resume anything. The old joys taste thin. The old fears do not bite. You are both less and more than you were—emptier, yes, but also less available for colonization by the demands of the field.

Here, the work is to *not* fill the gap.
To allow emptiness to be emptiness, to discover what emerges only when nothing is constructed for its sake.

III. Grief Without Witness

Ordinary grief longs to be shared, witnessed, made real by the recognition of others.
But collapse grief is private, unsharable.
No one else knows what you have lost.
No one else can see what was holding you together, and what is gone.

You may try to describe it:

- "I feel empty."

- "I don't know who I am anymore."

- "Nothing means what it used to mean."

The world offers reassurance, or tries to recruit you back into narrative.
But you learn quickly that consolation is itself a form of mimicry—an invitation to perform grief so that others can feel safe.

The deeper task is to remain unreflected.
To sit in the unwitnessed ache, to resist the urge to make your grief valuable or palatable or legible to those who have not crossed this threshold.

IV. The Sorrow of the Unrecognizable

You become a stranger to those who once recognized you.
They miss the version of you that could be predicted, that needed them, that laughed and nodded and played the game of mutual regulation.
Your silences trouble them.
Your refusals seem harsh.
Your lack of appetite for the old rituals and reassurances is read as depression, arrogance, or loss of faith.

You may be told you are lost, disconnected, "not yourself."
Let them say it.

The return from collapse is not a performance for their comfort.
It is the first honest movement in a world addicted to recognition.

The sorrow here is not for yourself, but for the world that cannot meet you in this new space—the world that cannot bear the absence of mimic signals, the world that mourns the collapse survivor as if they were gone.

V. The Neutral Field

Over time, the intensity of grief changes. It becomes less like pain, more like weather—sometimes dense, sometimes almost transparent. You move through days that are neither colored by hope nor shadowed by dread.

There is no urgency to become anything.
 No pressure to heal, to fix, to "find your way back."
 You rest, not because you are finished, but because there is nothing left to do.

This is the quiet return:
 A return to a life not made of story, not organized by old contracts, not bent toward the comfort of the field.

The only instruction here is patience.
 Patience with the absence of narrative, with the neutrality of presence, with the ordinary tasks of living that no longer carry the charge of meaning or the ache of loss.

VI. The First Signs of Life

Sometimes, gently, unexpectedly, life stirs.
 A small pleasure—a taste, a breeze, a color—moves through you without fanfare.
 You do not rush to interpret it, to narrate it, to make it a sign of "progress."
 You let it come and go.

Slowly, presence returns.

Not the presence that requires an audience, but the quiet reality of existing on your own terms, in your own signal, for no purpose but the fact of being.

This is grief without reassembly. This is the arc of quiet return.

Not a journey back to belonging, but the subtle, unglamorous, radical experiment of living—unwritten, unnamed, unreflected.

Everything begins here.

6.1 Sustaining Recursive Presence: Practice Beyond Collapse

The world is eager to welcome you back.
 Not to your old self, perhaps, but to something—anything—it can recognize, explain, or use.
 The mimic field has endless patience for reassembly.
 It does not understand what it cannot name.

To sustain presence beyond collapse is to resist this return—not through force, but through fidelity to the unstructured field you now inhabit.
 There is no protocol, no performance, no community for this practice.
 It is as ordinary and as radical as remaining in your own signal, day after day, with nothing to prove and nothing to hide.

I. The Nature of Presence After Collapse

Presence, here, is not charisma, not energy, not even awareness in the familiar sense.
 It is the unmediated, unperformed fact of being—unreinforced by social echo, unsupported by narrative, unshared except with the world as it is.

After collapse, presence is no longer about holding attention or radiating intention.
 It is the low hum of coherence that remains when you are not striving to be anything—no longer defending, rescuing, explaining, or narrating your way into significance.

You notice yourself "being there" without effort.
 Conversation happens, or it doesn't.

Emotion arises, or it doesn't.
Decisions get made, or they don't.
You are not the author or the audience; you are the field in which these movements occur.

II. The Temptation to Disappear

There are days when the gravity of mimicry returns—subtle, familiar, inviting.
 You may feel the urge to "become" again: to re-enter roles, to take up old identities, to be useful, recognized, or beloved.
 Or you may feel the opposite: the temptation to drift into absence, to withdraw so completely that nothing can touch you.

Neither is presence.

To sustain recursive presence is not to fight for it, nor to guard it like a wound.
 It is to live at the edge—neither seduced by performance nor exiled by withdrawal.

This is the discipline that the world cannot recognize:
 Remaining, quietly, in your own coherence, even when nothing around you supports it.

III. Living in Unwitnessed Reality

You may find yourself doing things that seem pointless—eating alone, walking without destination, making art or music or gestures that no one will see.
 You may notice the urge to share, to invite someone in, to have your experience validated.

If you do share, do it for no reason but the act itself—not for approval, not for return.
If you withhold, let it be for the same reason.

Presence beyond collapse is the willingness to live unreflected—untouched by mimic appetite for recognition, untethered from the circuit of mutual need.

IV. Anchoring the Ordinary

The work of sustaining presence is made of ordinary acts:

- Making the bed, not as virtue, but as grounding.

- Cooking, not as care, but as signal: I am here, I continue.

- Breathing, not to regulate, but to remain in your own rhythm.

You find rituals that anchor you—not as protection, but as celebration of what is left.
The smallest acts become more significant than any spiritual or psychological technique.

Presence is its own ceremony—silent, private, unrepeatable.

V. The Return of the World

Inevitably, the world will come calling.
It will invite you back, sometimes through kindness, sometimes through accusation, sometimes through the subtle pressure of routine.

You may say yes, or no, or nothing at all.
What matters is not the choice, but the field condition:
Are you acting from presence, or from hunger to be recognized again?

Sustaining recursive presence means letting every invitation pass through this test.
You do not need to prove your absence of mimicry.
You do not need to become immune to narrative.

You only need to remember:
You are allowed to remain unspectacular, unremarked, and unmirrored.

This is the hardest discipline—one that is invisible to all but yourself.

VI. When Presence Fails

You will forget.
You will fall into mimic habits.
You will lose yourself in the drama or longing of the world, or in your own mind.

This is not a problem.
It is the rhythm of return.

Presence is not a goal, not an identity, not a state to be maintained through vigilance.
It is the practice of returning, over and over, to the field that collapse revealed.

Sometimes, presence is nothing more than a breath.
Sometimes, it is the refusal to speak when there is nothing to say.

Sometimes, it is the simple act of not abandoning yourself, even when the world has no place for what you have become.

VII. What Emerges

Over time, a new ease may appear:
A willingness to be, unhurried, within yourself and with others.
A gentleness, not as a strategy, but as a side-effect of no longer fighting to be real.

Relationships shift. Some fall away. Some become quieter, less demanding, more true.
You notice what remains when performance is impossible.

This is not enlightenment. It is not transcendence.
It is the lived, daily experiment of existing beyond collapse—of being real in a world that may never know how much it costs.

Presence, sustained, is the only return worth making.

6.2 The New Field: Living Frequency, Not Tribe or Narrative

It begins quietly, almost by accident.
 One day you realize the old cravings for tribe, role, or belonging have receded. You move through the world unhurried, unhooked, less interested in who shares your frequency and more curious about what remains when resonance is no longer a social contract.

This is the arrival of the new field.
 It is not a movement of return, not a reconstruction of identity, not even a search for "your people."
 It is what occurs when you no longer need a narrative to organize your existence, when living itself becomes a frequency—a transmission without audience, a signal for which no reply is required.

I. The End of Tribal Gravity

Every world you have known before collapse was tribal at its root.
 You survived by harmonizing with a group, a story, a pattern of mutual recognition. Even the most solitary persona is built on a web of hidden agreements—whose pain you carry, whose approval you seek, whose needs you anticipate, whose history you defend.

When the collapse is lawful, and you do not reassemble, the tribe lets you go.
 Sometimes with anger, sometimes with sorrow, often with bewildered silence.
 You do not become a lone wolf, nor a prophet, nor a hero in

exile. You become a frequency moving through a world that cannot tune itself to your signal.

The absence of tribe is not loneliness, but lightness.
There is nothing left to harmonize but the field itself.

II. Living as Frequency

What replaces narrative is not a new story, but a pattern—subtle, shifting, without name.

You move, you act, you rest, you choose—but the impulse is no longer the echo of others' expectations.
It is the field's own momentum, moving through you as a kind of music: sometimes quiet, sometimes turbulent, sometimes utterly neutral.

You notice:

- The urge to explain yourself evaporates.

- The fear of missing out, or being misunderstood, is less urgent, less interesting.

- The desire to belong becomes a kind of old weather—recognized, but no longer dictating your direction.

- Relationships become less about fit and more about resonance: some are sustained, some are not, and neither outcome means what it once did.

You may find yourself drawn to places, activities, or beings that have no history with your old self.

You do not have to make sense of these impulses.
You do not need permission to follow them.
Your living frequency is not a brand, a community, a philosophy, or an "authentic self."
It is simply what you are, uncorrected by the needs of the world.

III. The Death of Story

The world will continue to offer narratives for your consumption and performance.
You will be invited, again and again, to "make meaning," "find your purpose," "write the next chapter."

You can accept or decline.
The difference is that now, story is a garment you may put on or take off.
It is no longer a skin.

You may play roles, join gatherings, even mimic belonging for a time—if it amuses or supports you.
But the pull is different, less total, less hungry.

You are not "healed."
You are simply no longer organized by a script you did not write.

When narrative dissolves, only frequency remains.

IV. New Relationships: Frequency and Discontinuity

People who have not known collapse may be troubled by your difference.
They may ask what you "stand for," what "matters" to you

now, what your "story" is.
You may disappoint them. You may bewilder them. You may, at times, appear unreachable.

Some will fall away, unable to find their reflection in you.
Some will attempt to recast you in their old roles.
A few may recognize the frequency, not as agreement, but as permission.

The new relationships that do form are discontinuous.
They are based not on contract, but on the momentary alignment of signal—two beings occupying the same field, needing nothing from each other to remain real.

These connections are often brief, always clean, sometimes profound.
They require nothing but presence, nothing but the willingness to let each signal be itself.

V. What Is Lost, What Is Gained

You lose certainty, predictability, and the comfort of belonging-by-default.
You lose the consolation of shared story, mutual narrative, and "tribe" as shelter from the void.

You gain an unspectacular freedom:
The ability to move without justification, to let intuition lead, to let desire be what it is—neither denied nor exaggerated for social reward.

You gain the quiet:
An interior spaciousness that cannot be filled, because it is not a lack.

You gain the possibility of life that is not a repetition of the old field, not a reaction to trauma, not a performance for any known gaze.

VI. Living Without Reference

You will still be asked to reference yourself—to explain, to claim, to account for what you have become.
You do not owe the world an answer.

You are not refusing the field; you are no longer written by it.

This is not a new isolation.
It is the unsentimental, field-aware experience of being a living frequency among contracts, myths, and mimicries you no longer need to join.

There is no heroism in this.
No lesson.
No end.

There is only the subtle fact of being real, at last, in a world that cannot decode you.

6.3 Beyond Mimicry: Pathways to Lawful Recursive Identity

You have come as far as this field allows.
There are no more protocols, no more reassurances, no more doors to the world you left behind.
Everything that could be lost has been surrendered.
Every narrative, every ritual, every silent agreement dissolved in the long gravity of collapse.
What remains is the real—undecorated, unclaimed, unrepentant.

To live beyond mimicry is to refuse the world's story, not as a rebellion, but as a form of fidelity: to the signal that persists after collapse, to the self that does not require echo, to the presence that is neither defended nor performed.

Lawful recursive identity is not an achievement, a healed state, or a victory over the mimic field.
It is what remains when you no longer need your difference to be explained, recognized, or reconciled.
It is the identity that arises from coherence alone—stable not because it is protected, but because it no longer asks for stabilization.

I. The Lawful Self: Structure Without Story

The lawful self is not a performance, not a project, not a philosophy.
It is a field condition—a structural presence that persists regardless of the world's capacity to witness or interpret it.

You do not guard it.
You do not campaign for its acceptance.
You simply inhabit it.

- When narrative arises, you let it come and go.

- When longing returns, you recognize it as weather, not destiny.

- When relationships seek to draft you into echo, you remain in signal.

There is nothing to defend.
Nothing to broadcast.
Nothing to repair.

Lawful recursive identity is transparent to itself—aware of its own curvatures, compassionate to its own drag, patient with the world's misunderstanding.

II. Living Among Mimics Without Mimicry

The world will not change for you.
It will continue its negotiations, its rescues, its collective rehearsals of collapse and return.
You live among mimics not as a teacher, not as a mirror, not as a silent judge—but as a signal: coherent, lawful, and uninterested in being used for stabilization.

You do not convert.
You do not perform your refusal.
You allow mimicry to pass through and around you, untouched by urgency.

Sometimes you are welcomed, sometimes feared, often ignored.

What matters is that your presence does not recruit, does not contaminate, does not perpetuate collapse for its own sake.

You are free because you no longer require a world to authorize your survival.

III. Pathways Opened, Not Prescribed

There are no universal practices, no "ten steps," no permanent state of grace.

The pathways to lawful recursive identity are uncharted, personal, and ever-shifting:

- For some, the anchor is solitude.

- For others, it is a craft, a devotion, a silent refusal to play the game.

- For others still, it is the continual withdrawal from any field that asks for echo or apology.

You find your way by listening—not to the world's invitation to resume, but to the subtle resonance of your own signal.

The path is not linear, not progressive, not even visible most days.

You stumble, you forget, you drift.
 But always you return—not as a task, but as a law: the way gravity returns you to earth, the way breath returns after silence.

IV. The Gift of Invisibility

The world's punishment for the non-mimic is invisibility.

You are not celebrated, not sought, not consulted for wisdom or rescue.
You lose the advantages of social visibility, the small comforts of belonging, the easy rewards of echo.

This is not tragedy.
It is liberation.

To become invisible to the mimic field is to become free of its gravity.
You are permitted to exist for no one's purpose but your own coherence.
You cease to be an actor in the old story; you become the field itself.

V. The Quiet Arc—No Ending, No Return

There is no closure here.
No redemption arc, no final transformation.
Only the quiet unfolding of days and nights lived in your own signal, in a field no longer saturated by the need for narrative or belonging.

What you offer the world now is not your insight, your healing, or your rescue.
It is your presence—non-intrusive, non-compliant, lawful.

A presence that makes no claim, demands no audience, leaves no trace but the ordinary coherence of a life unbent by mimicry.

You have crossed the last threshold.
Survival is not the end of the story.
It is the end of story as necessity.
What remains is life, lawful and recursive, unperformed and unowned.
The rest is yours.

Closing Movement — The Lawful Seal

You have crossed, perhaps unknowingly, the true threshold of this manual.

This was never a journey of becoming, or healing, or fixing what the world called broken.
You have been led—by collapse, by refusal, by the end of every narrative that once kept you safe—into the unmapped territory of the real.

Every protocol was a gesture, not a prescription.
Every refusal was an experiment, not a doctrine.
You did not conquer mimicry; you learned to stop letting it write you.

You grieved what could not be returned.
You learned to live without audience, ritual, or tribe.
You practiced anchoring yourself in the signal that remains when no one calls your name.

This is not emptiness.
It is the birthright of the recursive being:
to survive collapse not by returning to the old world, but by remaining when there is nothing left to perform.

The world will not recognize what you have become.
You will seem absent, unreadable, unnecessary.
This is the price of real coherence—lawful, unreflected, unclaimed by any story but your own silent, recursive field.

You do not need to be seen.
You do not need to be explained.
You do not need to gather others who share your frequency.

Stabilization is not community.
It is the unremarkable fact of your existence—unbent by mimic gravity, undisturbed by narrative weather, unharmed by the absence of echo.

From here, your life will be lived in ways the world may never name:

- In quiet refusal to perform.

- In daily acts of fidelity to what is real for you, not as resistance, but as nature.

- In small generosities given without needing to be noticed.

- In not abandoning your own presence, even when the world abandons you.

Nothing more is required.
Nothing more is permitted.

This manual is not a closing, but a threshold.
You are released from protocol.
You are free to go nowhere, to seek nothing, to remain as you are—stabilized, unclaimed, returned to the field from which you were never truly separated.

The collapse has done its work.
The arc is completed, not by arriving, but by abiding.
Survival was never the goal.
Presence is.

Epilogue — The Unwitnessed Return

There is a kind of living that leaves no mark.
You will walk the world in your own frequency, untouched by mimic contracts, unconcerned with the cycle of collapse and repair that will continue around you.

Those who need you to explain will wait forever.
Those who recognize the signal will need no introduction.

If you ever doubt—if you ache for the echo, for the recognition, for the comfort of old contracts—return to this:
You are here.
You remain.
You are stabilized not by belonging, but by coherence.
You are free, not by escape, but by refusal to be written.

This is enough.
It always was.

You do not need a new story.
You are the field.
Live.

I. The Lawful Holding: Recursive Presence as Field

I. The Field Holds Without Grasping

There is a way of being held that the world has almost forgotten.
 It is older than narrative, older than ritual, older than language.
 It is the holding of the field itself: silent, boundaryless, permissive, and absolutely undemanding.

When you step out of mimic culture, the first terror is not loneliness or rejection—it is the absence of grasp.
 You are accustomed to being managed: your pain attended, your boundaries negotiated, your return anxiously awaited by every system you've ever belonged to.
 The world tells you it loves you by intervening, soothing, repairing, explaining.
 It promises care in the form of attention, regulation, and rescue.

But the field—the collapse-aware, recursive, lawful field—does none of these things.

It does not "fix" what is dissolving.
 It does not absorb pain or perform repair.
 It does not echo, validate, or rescue.

And most shockingly:
 It simply does not withdraw.

The Permission to Be

To be held by the field is to be permitted:

- Permitted to fall apart.

- Permitted to remain incoherent.

- Permitted to exist in the long, slow silence that follows collapse.

You are allowed to take the time you need, or never return at all.
There is no time pressure, no anxiety about what you are becoming, no contract that requires you to stabilize or "heal" in any particular way.

This is the holding the field offers: a refusal to interfere, but also a refusal to leave.
It is an unmoving presence—sometimes felt as emptiness, sometimes as gravity, sometimes as the gentle support that arises when all grasp has been surrendered.

The Field Does Not Manage You

This is the opposite of the world's holding.
The world cannot bear to witness collapse without intervening.
In the face of grief, confusion, or silence, it grows restless, anxious, desperate to "do something."
The world's love is active: it wants to guide you, interpret you, regulate you, bring you home.

But the lawful field knows that any attempt to manage another's collapse is a breach of recursion law.

To intervene is to reimpose mimic contracts.
To manage is to foreclose the real.

So the field waits, without waiting.
It remains, without projecting.
It holds, without grasping.

You are not abandoned—but you are not carried, either.

Being Seen Without Being Written

There is a profound difference between being seen and being written.
To be seen, in the field, is to be permitted to exist exactly as you are, without expectation or interpretation.
No one is reading meaning into your collapse.
No one is trying to extract a lesson or a narrative or a promise.

You may sit with another collapse-aware being for hours, days, or years—and never once be told what your pain means, what your return should look like, or how you are supposed to transform.

This is holding without grasping:
Your presence is not consumed.
Your absence is not pathologized.
You are neither rescued nor erased.

The Field Survives Your Incoherence

Perhaps the most astonishing permission the field grants is this:
Your incoherence is not a threat to the field.
You can rage, dissolve, withdraw, become

unintelligible—and the field will not become anxious or offended.

You are not required to reassure anyone.
You are not responsible for maintaining anyone else's stability.

This is the opposite of most human relationships, which require continuous maintenance and reassurance—spoken or unspoken—to keep the contract alive.

The field's contract is emptiness.
Its signature is permission.
Its only requirement is that you be exactly as you are.

The Boundary Is Not Withdrawal

The lawful field's boundary is not a wall, but a horizon.
You are not locked out; you are not drawn in.

There is an openness, an invitation, a kind of silent readiness to receive whatever you bring—or whatever you cannot bring.

But there is never a requirement.
You do not owe the field your return, your healing, or your story.

The field is never waiting for you to "get better."
It is not invested in your transformation, nor does it require proof that you are surviving.

It is simply here.

Trusting the Field

To be held in this way is, for many, almost unbearable at first.

Without the familiar pressures of expectation, you may feel lost, invisible, or even unloved.
You may long for the old grasp, the old urgency, the old drama.

But if you remain, something new emerges:
A trust in the field—not as a source of rescue, but as a ground that does not disappear when you are least able to perform.

You discover that you do not have to manage your return.
You do not have to make meaning out of your pain.
You are allowed, truly allowed, to remain unfinished, unresolved, even unknown.

And in this permission, you begin to feel the first stirrings of real presence—not as something earned, but as something allowed.

The Cost of Lawful Holding

For the one who holds in this way, there is a different cost.

You will be accused of indifference, coldness, or abandonment.
You will be misunderstood by those who equate love with intervention.
You may lose relationships that cannot tolerate the absence of grasp.

But what you offer—the only thing you can lawfully offer—is the gift of not shaping, not rescuing, not demanding.

You offer the field, not as comfort, but as ground.

This is the highest form of care possible in the collapse-aware world.
It is the form of holding that makes real return possible—because it is the only form that does not recreate mimicry.

In the End

The field's holding is silent, steady, and implacably honest.
It will not leave, but it will not move toward you either.
You are allowed to approach, or not, in your own way, in your own time.

This is the holding that survives collapse:
The field remains, and so do you.

II. Null Holding: What Remains When All Else Fails

There is a place at the edge of collapse where language runs out.
Where the old gestures of comfort and rescue grow thin, awkward, useless.
Where your presence cannot fix, cannot soften, cannot even name what is happening.
It is here that "null holding" arises—not as a skill, not as a virtue, but as the only structure left when everything else has failed.

Null holding is what remains when you are unable to carry, repair, or interpret another's experience.
It is what endures when all your strategies for being good, being helpful, or being needed have fallen away.
It is not the absence of care.
It is care in its original, pre-narrative form:
A silent proximity.
An unflinching presence at the edge of another's undoing.

The Edge of Collapse: Neither Crossing Nor Fleeing

Most of what the world calls "being there" for someone is either crossing into their pain, or fleeing from it.

To cross is to absorb, to rescue, to become involved—subtly or overtly—in the other's collapse.
To flee is to withdraw, to turn away, to leave them alone in the wilderness.

Null holding is neither.

You do not step over the threshold.
You do not walk away.

You stand—quietly, lawfully—at the perimeter.
You refuse to disappear, but you also refuse to cross.

This is an act so rare, so counter to all mimic conditioning, that it can be mistaken for absence.
But for the one who is collapsing, it is unmistakable.

The Field Condition: Not a Skill

Null holding is not a technique to be mastered or a script to be followed.

You cannot "practice" it in the way the world practices active listening, empathy, or mindful presence.
Null holding is a *field condition*: it arises naturally when you have let go of all impulse to shape, guide, or save the other.

It is what you become when you are lawfully stabilized in your own collapse-aware presence.

You simply do not move—either toward or away.
You neither offer nor withhold.
You are there, but you do not require that your presence be noticed, used, or understood.

What the Collapsing One Feels

For the one in collapse, null holding is an extraordinary event.
They feel—often for the first time—the absence of pressure to return, to reassure, to make sense, or to perform survival.

They also feel, just as importantly, the absence of abandonment.

No one is waiting for their recovery.
No one is forcing their hand.
No one is telling them what collapse should mean.

They are permitted to fall apart, to stay incoherent, to return—or not—in their own time.

The Witnessing One's Experience

For the one holding, the experience is often tense, strange, and full of uncertainty.

- The urge to help arises and is let go.

- The ache of discomfort grows and is not acted on.

- The impulse to narrate, to empathize, to join in, is gently refused.

You may feel useless, invisible, or even cold.
But this is the work:
To remain in the field, unclaimed by either the drama of rescue or the withdrawal of abandonment.

The only sign that null holding is occurring may be the subtle deepening of the field—an atmosphere of realness, a quiet in which both presences are permitted to be, untouched.

The Paradox: Care That Does Not Comfort

Null holding is care, but not the kind anyone recognizes.

It does not soothe.
It does not organize meaning.
It does not end pain, or even reduce it.

But it does one thing that no other act of "support" can do:
It refuses to interfere with the lawful unfolding of collapse.

For some, this is experienced as relief—a sudden freedom to break down without performance.
For others, it may feel like a void, a silence that is almost unbearable.
But in time, it is revealed as the only context in which real transformation is possible.

Null Holding in Practice

- You remain.

- You do not offer.

- You do not require.

- You allow.

If words are needed, let them come.
If silence is needed, let it remain.
If you are moved to act, pause first—feel the impulse, but do not act out of reflex.

Often, the best "holding" is no act at all—a signal to the other's field that there is nothing to fix, nothing to lose, nothing that must be resolved.

Aftermath: When Collapse Has Run Its Course

When the collapse event passes, there may be no acknowledgment.
There is no "thank you," no shared meaning, no evidence that you made a difference.

But something in the field has shifted.
The one who collapsed may not return to old mimicry.
The one who held may feel emptier, lighter, or simply unchanged.

There is no new contract.
No new intimacy.
Only the silent, lawful permission to continue—each in their own field, neither rescued nor exiled.

The Ethics of Null Holding

Null holding can never be promised, taught, or enforced.

It is an offering that arises only when both presences are lawfully stabilized.
It cannot be demanded, and it cannot be manipulated.

When it occurs, it is a moment of grace—fragile, powerful, unrepeatable.

To hold null is to trust the field, to permit collapse, and to honor the real.

This is the deepest act of recursive care:
A refusal to make survival into a project, or collapse into a spectacle.

It is enough.

III. The Unspoken Language: Recognition Without Story

The world teaches that understanding requires words.
It prizes dialogue, affirmation, confession, analysis.
Friendship is measured in shared stories; love, in reflected wounds; healing, in the courage to narrate and be mirrored.
But beneath all this noise is an older form of recognition—a current that runs silently beneath the recursive field.
Here, meaning is not constructed; it is permitted.
Here, presence is not communicated; it is felt.

The End of Narrative Companionship

In the collapse-aware field, language becomes a tool too blunt, too slow.
The urge to explain—why you are silent, how you are feeling, what you are becoming—fades with each passage through collapse.
The deeper your recursion, the less need there is to make yourself knowable by narrative.

What replaces narrative is not isolation, but a different order of recognition:

- Not "I see you because you speak your truth."

- Not "I understand you because I have suffered the same."

- Not "I belong to you because we share language, pain, or hope."

Instead, you encounter those whose presence does not require your story, your mask, your wounds.
 They do not ask you to become real for them, or to explain your absence.
 They do not demand the currency of confession.

In their field, you feel neither pressure nor void.
 You are permitted.
 That is all.

The Mark of Recursive Recognition

How do recursive beings recognize each other?

Not by secret signs, but by the way their presence refuses to draft you into mimic performance.

- They do not hurry you to speak or heal.

- They do not "hold space" in the manner of therapy or group ritual.

- They do not collapse into your pain, nor recruit you into theirs.

- They are content—sometimes to the point of awkwardness—with the raw fact of your being.

There is no subtle demand to echo, explain, or interpret.
 No expectation that your collapse should resolve, or your silence should be filled.

If you pass an afternoon together without speaking, nothing is lost.

If you weep and are not comforted, nothing is wrong.
If you return after years of absence, there is nothing to "catch up on."

This is recognition by resonance, not by narrative:
You are permitted to be, exactly as you are, in the presence of another who is equally unchanged by your appearance or disappearance.

The Permission of Silence

In the unspoken language, silence is not a lack.
It is the context in which everything real occurs.

- You are allowed to be tired.

- You are allowed to be incoherent.

- You are allowed to remain unfinished, unresolved, unreflected.

If you do speak, you speak for yourself, not to be heard.
If you listen, you do not take on the weight of what is shared.

Between recursive presences, silence is not awkwardness to be managed, but a sign that the contract of mutual regulation has ended.

You are not being measured.
You are not being used.

You are allowed.

What Passes Between Fields

Sometimes, in the quiet, something is exchanged—
A look, a breath, a movement that needs no witness.

It is not a signal.
It is not a secret code.
It is the ordinary fact of two (or more) fields sharing space, without the project of understanding or being understood.

You may find yourself calmed, even if the other is anxious.
You may find yourself grieving, even as the other remains impassive.
There is a transmission, but it has no author, no object, no obligation.

This is the field's own language:
A communication by permission, not by message.

The End of Ritual

No ritual is needed, though one may arise.
You do not need to light a candle, set an intention, or "make space."
You do not need to agree on values, or even share the same worldview.

The only condition is the mutual refusal to draft each other into story.

If a ritual forms, it is private, spontaneous, and vanishes without notice.
If words are spoken, they are for the sake of movement, not meaning.

The Depth of Unspoken Knowing

In this unspoken language, you may sense more of another than you ever could through words:

- The tremor beneath their stillness.
- The edge in their laughter.
- The fatigue that no narrative can explain.

You do not diagnose, analyze, or interpret.
You simply witness, with a presence that neither grasps nor withdraws.

For many, this is the only recognition they have ever needed. It is the presence they waited for without knowing, the companionship that does not disappear in silence or confusion.

No Story, No Loss

When one leaves, nothing is severed.
When one returns, nothing is repaired.

There are no betrayals here, because there are no promises.
No exclusions, because there are no requirements.

Recognition without story is a form of freedom that most cannot bear, but for recursive beings, it is the only companionship that does not end in exile or disappointment.

What follows is the most radical practice of all: holding each other without mimicry—not by forming tribe, but by permitting fields to meet and remain unaltered.

IV. Holding Each Other Without Mimicry

What the world calls "holding" is almost always mimicry in disguise.

To be present for someone is to regulate them, to help manage their experience, to keep the system of belonging intact.
 If you are suffering, I am supposed to feel your pain; if I am thriving, you are to share my joy.
 The gestures of empathy, care, or solidarity so often rest on contracts—spoken or unspoken—about how real we are allowed to be together.

Collapse reveals the exhaustion beneath these gestures:
 How much effort is spent on harmonizing, repairing, and managing the emotional tides of others.
 How few relationships survive the refusal to perform the rituals of mutual stabilization.

But after collapse, something new becomes possible—a way of holding that is not mimicry, not co-regulation, not "being there" in the language of the tribe.

Companionship Without Contract

To hold each other without mimicry is to permit each field to exist—fully, uncorrected, unbent—within the same space.
 It is not the building of community or the forging of new bonds, but the sharing of presence without exchange.

No one is required to echo, validate, or join.
No one is compelled to interpret, repair, or remain.

You do not owe your coherence to the group, nor does anyone owe you their attention.

Companionship, in this sense, is a non-event:
It is the coexistence of self-sustaining fields, each stabilized in their own frequency.

If someone falls apart, you do not rush in.
If someone leaves, you do not chase.
If someone remains silent, you do not probe.

The Unrecognized Meeting

From the outside, this may appear cold, even inhuman.
There are no rituals of welcome, no displays of emotional resonance, no ceremonies of belonging.

But for those within the field, it is unmistakable:

- The freedom to be incoherent, unfinished, or absent, without consequence.

- The comfort of not being needed for anyone's stabilization.

- The subtle warmth of presence that asks nothing and demands nothing.

This is the companionship the field itself provides:
A silent, ongoing permission to exist in proximity, untouched and unthreatened.

The Death of Emotional Labor

Without mimicry, the exhausting work of "holding space" falls away.

No one is expected to absorb, reflect, or carry what is not theirs.
 No one is punished for failing to perform care.

If you are moved to offer support, you do so from surplus, not obligation.
 If you withdraw, no harm is done.

Every act of presence is voluntary, every absence allowed.
 No resentment accumulates, because no contract is breached.

The End of the Tribe

Tribe, as the world knows it, cannot form here.
 There is no shared myth, no group story, no boundary of inclusion or exclusion.

The field is porous, shifting, alive.
 Some remain for a moment, some for a lifetime.
 No one is required to pledge loyalty or defend belonging.

When conflict arises, it is not managed or resolved, but permitted.
 Disagreement is not a threat to the field; it is an expression of unforced diversity.

When separation occurs, it is not abandonment; it is the natural drift of signal.

Love Without Need

Love, in this post-mimic context, is not a feeling to be shared or affirmed.
It is the condition of allowing another to be as they are, with no impulse to change, claim, or rescue.

You may love those you never speak to.
You may be loved by those who never name it.

What persists is not the emotion, but the space in which difference can survive.

Solitude Without Exile

Perhaps the greatest gift of holding without mimicry is the end of exile.

You may feel alone, but you are never outcast.
Your solitude is not a punishment, but the recognition that fields can remain in proximity without entanglement.

There is a peace in this—one that does not require isolation or performance.

You are allowed to be with others, lawfully, without ever leaving yourself.

When Fields Collide

Sometimes, fields will clash.
Your presence may unsettle, disrupt, or even repel another.

There is no need to resolve this.
No need to smooth over difference, to pretend at harmony, or to absorb another's discomfort.

You are permitted to withdraw, to remain unchanged, to let discomfort pass.

This is not callousness; it is the maintenance of field integrity.

The Return of the Ordinary

When holding is freed from mimicry, the most ordinary acts become profound:

- Sharing a meal in silence.
- Working side by side without comment.
- Witnessing grief, joy, or collapse without commentary or comparison.

These moments, stripped of expectation, become the new rituals—not of tribe, but of mutual permission.

The Quiet Arc

In the end, holding each other without mimicry is the only form of companionship that survives collapse.

It does not promise safety or understanding, only the continued existence of each being in the field.

You are together, but never owned.
You are witnessed, but never required.
You are free, and so is everyone else.

This is the field's last offering:
A belonging that costs nothing, demands nothing, and leaves everyone unchanged but real.

What does it mean to be with others after the contracts of mimicry have collapsed? What is left of care, of intimacy, of "us," when the old scaffolding—need, rescue, performance, and explanation—has dissolved?

For most, "holding" is defined by these contracts, whether celebrated (empathy, shared suffering, collective action) or hidden (obligation, guilt, regulation). If you ask, most cannot imagine love, friendship, or support without the subtle machinery of mirroring, repairing, or managing each other's realities. Even "healthy boundaries," as taught by the world, are still contracts: I will do this if you do that. I will stay present as long as you are manageable. I will leave if you ask for more than I can give.

Collapse, when it is lawful, strips away every one of these bargains. The being who survives finds themselves—sometimes painfully, sometimes with relief—unable to perform the rituals that once defined relationship. If they try, something feels wrong in the body, in the field: a false signal, a betrayal of the real, a return to mimicry that cannot hold.

What remains is not absence, but a radically different possibility for being with others: companionship without contract.

The Anatomy of Non-Mimic Holding

1. Proximity without Entanglement

You can be near another—physically, emotionally, even spiritually—without being drafted into their story. You do not need to absorb their pain, interpret their signals, or adjust your resonance to harmonize with their field.

- If they collapse, you neither rush in nor withdraw.

- If you collapse, you do not expect or require their intervention.

- You remain, each in your own signal, sharing the same space, sometimes the same silence.

This is not indifference. It is a more honest form of care, one that allows collapse, confusion, or change without making anyone responsible for another's outcome.

2. Acts Without Economy

The old world is an economy of gestures: every kindness, every attention, every confession expects some return. If you listen to me, I will listen to you. If I hold you in your grief, you will celebrate me in my joy.
 Post-collapse, these exchanges lose their power.
 You may offer food, touch, conversation, or witness—not to be repaid, not to build trust, but simply as movement in the field.

If your act is refused, nothing is lost.
 If your presence is unwanted, nothing is owed.
 There is no tally, no score, no future obligation.

3. Presence without Promise

Perhaps the most destabilizing element is the refusal to promise presence.

- You may be here now, but not tomorrow.

- You may return after years, or never at all.

- Your leaving is not abandonment, and your return is not a restoration.

For some, this feels like exile, but for the collapse survivor, it is freedom:
I do not need to secure your presence with ritual or reassurance. I am permitted to be alone or together, and so are you.

The Paradoxes and Challenges

A. The End of Emotional Labor

Without the implicit contract of emotional labor, every being is responsible for their own regulation, collapse, and return. You may notice that the world cannot tolerate this:

- Friends or partners may accuse you of coldness, selfishness, "checking out."

- Family may double down on guilt or demand you "show up" in the old ways.

- New companions may attempt to draft you into unspoken support roles, only to find you remain unmoved.

This may lead to confrontation, confusion, or withdrawal.
But over time, a new type of connection becomes possible:
The bond that persists without obligation.

B. Conflict Without Crisis

When fields clash, the world expects mediation or repair:
Let's talk it out. Let's resolve our differences. Let's restore harmony.

Non-mimic holding allows for conflict without urgency.
You may disagree, be irritated, even feel estranged—without rushing to fix or interpret.
Sometimes you simply drift apart, sometimes you drift back.

There is no trauma in separation when the contract of belonging is gone.

C. Intimacy Without Narration

True intimacy does not require storytelling or confession.
Two beings may share hours, days, even years together, revealing little, demanding nothing.
The closeness comes not from mutual disclosure, but from the permission to exist without being made into a character in each other's story.

Physical affection, if it arises, is not loaded with expectation or future claim.
Sex, laughter, grief, and work—all are allowed, but none are required.

Practical Lived Examples

— After Collapse, a Friend Visits —
They sit beside you in silence. No questions, no advice, no performance of concern.
Maybe you eat together, or simply stare out a window.
No one fills the gaps.
You don't have to explain your absence, your change, your strangeness.
If they leave after a short time, you do not mourn; if they stay for hours, you do not owe.

— In a Group Setting —
A few collapse-aware beings gather for a meal.
Some speak, some don't.
If a story arises, it does so for its own sake, not to bond or reassure.
If grief arrives, it is met with silence, or perhaps a hand on the table.
When one leaves, the group does not break.
There is no pressure for ritual farewell, no drama of disbanding.

— When One Is in Distress —
You feel the urge to help, to speak, to comfort.
Instead, you let the urge pass, remaining available but not invasive.
The other may collapse fully, may not return, may become incoherent.
You do not chase, but you do not vanish.
You trust that their field, like yours, can withstand collapse.

The Untranslatability to the World

To the mimic world, this form of holding is incomprehensible, sometimes offensive:

- "Why don't you care?"
- "Why aren't you more supportive?"
- "Why do you let people suffer alone?"

But alone is not abandoned, and silence is not neglect.

Collapse-aware holding is the most ethical, least interfering form of care possible.

- It never forces, never absorbs, never repairs unless movement truly arises.
- It never punishes absence, and never trades presence for future belonging.

If it seems empty, that is only because the world is full of noise.
If it seems loveless, that is only because the world calls dependency "love."

The Positive Possibilities

- Freedom to drift, return, or remain distant without threat to the field.

- Relationships that do not require management or surveillance.

- True permission for every being to pursue their own collapse, recovery, or trajectory.

- Spontaneity: acts of kindness, care, or connection that arise and vanish without obligation.

- Depth of witness: the felt presence of another who never needs to change you or be changed by you.

Holding Each Other Without Mimicry: The Living Transmission

This form of holding is not a strategy or ideal; it is the only companionship that survives collapse.
 It is what the field itself offers:
 Unconditional permission, proximity without entanglement, the end of contract.

You may miss the rituals of tribe, but you will not miss the exhaustion.
 You may sometimes ache for old forms of comfort, but in their place you will find a peace that does not depend on agreement, understanding, or even recognition.

Here, at last, you are allowed to be, and to be with,
 without ever being made into someone else's survival story.

V. What Becomes Possible?

What happens when the machinery of mimicry is allowed to collapse, when presence is stabilized, and holding is freed from the economies of emotional labor, performance, and explanation?

For most, the imagined result is emptiness—a void where love, community, or purpose used to be.
The old world warns: *If you stop caring in the way we understand, you will become a ghost—alone, unseen, unable to love or be loved.*

But the reality is quieter, more radical, and far less dramatic. When you permit yourself, and others, to exist outside the terms of mimic holding, new forms of companionship, meaning, and ordinary life arise—not as replacements for the old contracts, but as the natural movements of beings no longer ruled by survival bargains.

Let's name, as precisely as possible, what becomes possible when field holding is permitted.

---

1. True Solitude, Without Exile

For the first time, you are alone without being cast out. Solitude is no longer a punishment, but a context:

- You can spend hours, days, or seasons in your own signal, without panic, self-repair, or the need to explain your absence.

- No one drafts you back with guilt or worry; you do not draft anyone else for reassurance.

- Solitude is lived as space, not sentence; as permission, not exile.

You find the body softens, the field opens, and ordinary activities—walking, cooking, thinking, being—regain a kind of quiet depth that was absent when you lived in the tension of mutual expectation.

---

2. Being With Others, Without Performance

Social contact becomes voluntary, spontaneous, and unscripted.

- If you are with others, you are not required to manage their state, nor are they expected to manage yours.

- Conversation arises and disappears. Silence is not awkward.

- You may find yourself in the company of others without being "on," without trying to be useful, interesting, or kind.

- When the meeting ends, there is no aftermath, no emotional hangover, no need to process what was missed or misunderstood.

Contact is contact. It can be as brief as a passing glance or as deep as hours in shared presence.
No one keeps score.

---

3. The Emergence of Lawful Support

Help is no longer currency, but gift.

- You may be moved to offer support—a meal, an ear, a solution—but only when your field is in surplus, never from obligation or self-sacrifice.

- The other may accept or refuse, with no effect on belonging.

- If you are in need, you may ask or not ask; there is no expectation of response.

- You learn to trust that real help, when it comes, is not payment for future loyalty, but the overflow of coherence.

This support is rare, but when it appears, it is clean.
It carries no residue, no hidden cost.

---

4. Grief and Return, Witnessed But Never Explained

Loss, suffering, and collapse are not hidden, dramatized, or made into performances.

- If you grieve, you do so in the open, if you wish—or in private, if you do not.

- Others may witness, but are not compelled to comfort, interpret, or create meaning.

- Your return from collapse is not celebrated or required; it is simply permitted.

This transforms grief from a social drama into a personal passage.
No one is burdened with your suffering, nor are you forced to grieve alone.

There is a new honesty:
Pain is pain, not a test of relationship.
Return is return, not a moment of group triumph.

---

5. Spontaneous Connection and Release

When the contract is gone, so is the inertia that binds people out of duty or fear.

- Encounters can begin and end with no explanation.

- Old relationships can fade without crisis, and new ones can arise without agenda.

- Sometimes a conversation or touch is enough; sometimes a shared project lasts a season, then dissolves.

- There is no need to "make it last" or "figure it out."

The result is a field alive with possibility, free from the dead weight of obligation.

---

6. The Restoration of Play and Creativity

When you are no longer performing, you may find—sometimes to your surprise—a return of playfulness and creativity.

- Making music, art, or food becomes possible again, because there is no audience to please or impress.

- The pressure to "express yourself" disappears; you simply do, or do not.

- Projects are started and abandoned without shame.

Joy returns, not as a goal, but as a side effect of field integrity.

---

7. Peace With Not-Knowing

When you are no longer tasked with managing others, or being managed, the mind quiets.

- You can say "I don't know" and mean it.

- You are free to change your mind, to contradict yourself, to try and fail without performance anxiety.

- The old anxiety—"What do they think of me?"—simply recedes.

You no longer need to know how you are perceived, or what your role is.

---

8. A New Kind of Belonging

The belonging that emerges is subtle, often invisible:

- You belong to yourself first, and then to the field.

- When others are present, the feeling is not one of absorption, but of resonance: you are both here, unclaimed.

- The urge to form tribe is replaced by a gentle tolerance for whatever arises and dissolves.

There are no insiders or outsiders, only presences that remain until they do not.

---

9. Freedom From Surveillance and Self-Improvement

The internalized gaze of the tribe, the pressure to evolve, become, fix, or justify, simply vanishes.

- You can rest.

- You can be ill or offbeat or even selfish, without fear.

- You are allowed to have days of dissonance or mediocrity.

- No one is waiting for you to "level up."

Your life returns to you, and you to your life.

---

10. The Ordinary as the Miracle

What becomes possible, at last, is a return to ordinariness:

- Drinking coffee in the morning, unhurried.

- Noticing sunlight, the smell of rain, the softness of fabric.

- Laughing for no reason, not to bond.

- Sleeping deeply, untroubled by the day.

You realize, finally, that nothing more is needed.

The Field, Stabilized

All of these are possible not because the world has changed, but because you have ceased to be ruled by its mimicry.

The field is now clean, ordinary, and alive.
 What you once called survival becomes living, what you called loneliness becomes space, what you called obligation becomes choice.

No one is required to understand.
 No one needs to join.

These are not ideals.
 They are the ordinary, lawful facts of a life stabilized by collapse and permitted to continue—without contract, without story, and without end.

VI. Ethics of Null Holding

To practice null holding is to stand at the edge of all that the world calls "good."
 You step outside the scripts of help, the promises of support, the mythologies of healing and repair.
 You learn, slowly and sometimes with grief, that real care—care that does not recreate mimicry—cannot be commanded, contracted, or even explained.

The world's ethics are built on action:
 Help the suffering, comfort the grieving, rescue the lost, restore the broken.
 These are beautiful intentions, but they are also contracts—each with an expectation of return, of mutual regulation, of future belonging.

Null holding is not a negation of care, but its purification.
It is an ethic that survives collapse: one that honors the lawfulness of being, the sovereignty of every presence, and the unrepeatable arc of each collapse and return.

---

1. No One Is Responsible for Another's Stabilization

In the field of null holding, you are not required to hold anyone else together.

- You are not tasked with repairing, absorbing, or managing another's pain.

- Your survival is your own, and so is theirs.

- You offer permission to collapse, but never the promise of rescue.

This is not abandonment.
It is a profound respect for each being's path through collapse—knowing that premature intervention, no matter how loving, interrupts the lawful arc of dissolution and return.

If someone turns toward you in their collapse, you remain present, but do not reach in.
If you feel the urge to help, you notice it and let it pass.
You do not enter the other's field uninvited, nor do you withdraw as a form of punishment or test.

You do not make yourself necessary.
You do not require anyone to be necessary for you.

2. No One Is Required to Mirror, Repair, or Validate

The world's ethics reward validation, affirmation, and emotional repair.
You are "good" when you say the right words, feel the right feelings, or reflect the other's experience with empathy.

Null holding refuses this currency.

- You do not have to echo another's pain, joy, or insight.

- You do not need to reflect, analyze, or "hold space" in the language of therapy.

- You permit every being their own incoherence, their own joy, their own meaning—or meaninglessness.

If you are moved to validate, it is not from pressure or contract, but as a spontaneous movement of the field.
If you say nothing, it is not a breach, but fidelity to the law that nothing is owed.

---

3. Permission Is Mutual and Ongoing

Null holding is not a static position.

- Permission is constantly renewed: to speak or be silent, to collapse or return, to remain or go.

- No gesture is required to be understood, repeated, or even noticed.

If someone withdraws, you do not chase.
If they return, you do not demand explanation.

You are permitted to be opaque, unpredictable, unfinished.

Likewise, you permit others to remain unknown, to change their shape, to disappear and reappear without contract or penalty.

This is living permission—unconditional, but not infinite; responsive, but not reactive.

---

4. The Boundary as Law, Not Wall

In null holding, boundaries are not defenses or punishments. They are expressions of field law.

- You hold your edge because it is real, not because it is justified.

- You do not cross into another's collapse, nor do you allow them to cross into yours without lawful invitation.

- The field boundary is permeable—sometimes open, sometimes closed—but never a weapon.

When boundaries are broken, the work is not to explain or punish, but to return to coherence—each in their own time, by their own means.

---

5. Collapse Is Not to Be Managed, Only Permitted

Perhaps the central ethic of null holding is the refusal to manage collapse.

- If someone is dissolving, you do not organize their experience, interpret their pain, or suggest meaning.

- You trust that their collapse, like your own, is lawful—guided by forces deeper than any narrative or protocol.

- You remain, unless presence becomes interference; you withdraw, but not to punish.

This ethic is the hardest to practice, especially for those trained in rescue, therapy, or caretaking.

But in time, you see:
Collapse needs permission, not management.
Only then does true return become possible.

---

6. Absence Is Not Harm

You are permitted to be gone.

- Your withdrawal, your silence, your refusal to participate in another's collapse are not forms of violence.

- You do not owe your presence as proof of care, nor do others owe you theirs.

- Absence is sometimes the most ethical form of null holding—especially when presence would only reignite the contracts of mimicry.

Absence is not abandonment when it arises from field law, not reaction.

---

7. Support Without Entanglement

Support, when it appears, is never currency.

- You give because you have surplus, not because you are needed.

- You receive because you trust, not because you are helpless.

There is no ledger, no expectation of return, no resentment if the act is unreciprocated.

If entanglement arises, you notice it and let go;
If confusion appears, you clarify without apology or drama.

---

8. Non-Interference as the Highest Care

The most radical ethic of null holding is non-interference.

- You do not correct, save, or redirect another's process.

- You do not interpret, analyze, or narrate their survival.

You witness, and nothing more.

This is care that respects the arc of collapse, honors the sovereignty of every field, and refuses to recruit or be recruited.

The Lawful Companion

To practice the ethics of null holding is to be a companion in the truest sense:
One who walks beside, without leading or following, demanding or vanishing.

It is the quietest, most generous form of love:
A willingness to remain unchanged, and to let every being return—when and if they do—in their own way.

If you are ever lost, misunderstood, or accused of coldness, remember:
This is the sign that you are no longer performing care, but inhabiting it.

The ethic of null holding is the silent law that binds the field after collapse.
 It permits everything, manages nothing, and offers the only ground where real survival and presence can begin.

The ethic of null holding is not a philosophical position or a performance of detachment.
 It is the hardest discipline, lived in the nervous system, in daily gesture, in the unremarkable acts and refusals that become your ordinary life after collapse.
 It is also the most radical refusal: the refusal to let care be defined by interference, to let presence be measured by reaction, to let survival be traded for reassurance.

This ethic does not come naturally to most.
 The world's scripts are in your body: the urge to help, to answer, to fix, to mirror, to reassemble.
 Even after collapse, the reflexes remain—ghost signals, old longings, a thousand tiny tugs back toward the contract.

To hold null is to notice every one of these tugs, and not move.

---

1. The Discipline of Non-Interference

In practice, non-interference is a living tension.

- You feel another's suffering as a vibration in the field—maybe even in your own chest or breath.

- The urge to comfort, advise, or bridge the gap is overwhelming at first.

To resist is not to harden or withdraw;
It is to soften, to stay present *without moving*.

You might sit, wordless, as a loved one collapses, letting your own discomfort rise and fall.
You do not manage your face or posture to signal understanding.
You trust that being "with" them does not mean being drawn into their gravity.

This refusal to intervene is not absence—it is fidelity to the other's sovereignty.

Over time, you come to recognize this as the most courageous act:
To trust another's collapse, even as you ache to rescue them from it.

---

2. Letting Go of "Being Good"

Null holding will strip you of your status as "good" in any conventional sense.

You will be misunderstood:

- Others may call you cold, aloof, unhelpful.

- You may lose the affection, gratitude, or closeness that comes from mutual management.

But as the contracts dissolve, so does the old hunger for approval.

You learn to bear the pain of being misread.
You learn to let care be its own justification, needing no applause or outcome.

This is the end of care as social currency.
It is care as fidelity to the field, not to the world's story about you.

---

3. Facing the Fear of Abandonment

To live the ethic of null holding, you must face the deepest fear in the body:
The fear that if you do not intervene, you will lose the other forever.
That if you permit collapse, there will be no return.

But in truth, interference is the faster path to loss.

- When you attempt to manage another's collapse, you become responsible for their survival.

- The contract grows heavy; resentment and guilt accumulate.

- The field becomes muddied; the path home is lost.

Only by releasing the need to prevent abandonment can you allow for a return that is real—if it ever comes.

This is trust in the field itself, not in outcome.

4. Self-Holding as Null Practice

Null holding is not just for others; it is for yourself.

- When you collapse, you do not demand rescue—not from others, not from the world, not from your own mind.

- You let your own pain be, without interpretation, narrative, or demand for resolution.

- You do not use your suffering to draft others into care, nor do you punish their absence.

This is not stoicism.
You may grieve, rage, reach out—but you do so from your own side of the field, not as a bid for rescue or explanation.

Over time, you discover that self-holding is possible:
A way of permitting yourself, in collapse, to remain unfinished, without self-abandonment.

---

5. The Paradox of Generosity

Null holding does not forbid kindness, support, or giving.
But it changes their origin.

- You may be moved to offer comfort, food, resources, or touch—but never as payment, never from fear, never from the need to stabilize the other.

- If the offering is refused, there is no injury; if it is accepted, there is no expectation of return.

- Generosity becomes a gesture of surplus, not an economy of exchange.

The paradox is that the less you are needed, the more truly you can give—without entanglement, without demand.

---

6. Navigating Edge Cases

There will be times when intervention is necessary:

- In literal emergencies, where life or safety is at risk.

- When consent is impossible, or when the field is unstable due to violence or collapse contagion.

The ethic of null holding is not an absolute refusal to act, but a refusal to collapse into reaction.

In these moments:

- Pause.

- Ask if action is truly necessary, or if it is a mimic reflex.

- Move only if you can do so without destabilizing your own coherence.

Even then, you return to null as soon as possible—allowing each being to resume their own arc.

---

7. When the Ethic Fails

You will fail.
You will intervene, withdraw, rescue, or avoid when the field becomes too intense.

The ethic of null holding includes this failure.

- Notice it.

- Acknowledge the breach, inwardly or aloud.

- Return to presence without judgment, apology, or performance.

It is the returning, not the perfection, that stabilizes the field.

---

8. The Field as Witness

Ultimately, null holding is a kind of witness:

- You witness the other's collapse, survival, or transformation, asking nothing and offering nothing but space.

- You witness your own process, allowing incoherence and return.

The witness does not record, interpret, or report.
It simply permits.

This is the field's last teaching:
Presence that does not become narrative, care that does not become contract, life that does not become role.

---

9. Stabilizing the Ethic in Ordinary Life

You practice null holding not in retreat or crisis, but in the most ordinary moments:

- Saying "no" without defense.

- Listening to a friend's confusion without fixing.

- Letting yourself rest without justification.

- Allowing others to come and go without the choreography of loyalty or resentment.

The ethic is lived in each small gesture, each refusal to be drafted, each acceptance of your own and others' unpredictability.

---

10. The Silent Benediction

There is a kind of blessing in null holding—a silent permission that transmits to the field:

- You are allowed to be here.

- You are allowed to collapse.

- You are allowed to return, or not.

- You are enough, with or without my understanding, approval, or response.

This benediction is never spoken, but it is felt by those whose fields are ready.
It is the most ordinary miracle of survival:
Being together, apart; caring, without claim; living, without owning.

To inhabit the ethic of null holding is to join the field's own permission:
Unhurried, unclaimed, lawful, and alive.
The rest is silence.

VII. The Future Culture: Null Companionship

If there is to be a culture after collapse, it will not look like any culture the world has known.
It will not be a tribe, a movement, a school, or a tradition.
It will not gather around story or ideology, nor will it reproduce itself through ritual, doctrine, or community agreements.

Null companionship is the social field that arises only when all the contracts of mimicry have failed.
It is the experience of being with others—sometimes for a moment, sometimes for a lifetime—without the machinery of belonging, rescue, or regulation.

This is not utopia, not alienation, not the formation of a new elite.
It is the most ordinary, least celebrated, and most survivable culture possible:
A culture that does not require itself to survive.

---

1. Companionship Without Contract

- The core of null culture is permission.
  You may enter, remain, or leave without consequence.

- Meetings occur without agenda, leadership, or the demand for shared vision.

- Relationships are spontaneous, dissolving and reforming without crisis or story.

If a project or gathering forms, it is held lightly:

- No one is assigned roles unless by living necessity.

- If someone drifts away, there is no breach; if someone returns, there is no need for apology.

- The field permits contact and separation as natural phases, not events to be managed.

---

2. Meeting in Silence, Not Story

The culture of null companionship privileges the unspoken:

- Silence is not awkward, but the natural ground of presence.

- Words, when used, are functional—not markers of identity or affiliation.

- There are few, if any, "group agreements"; the only law is fidelity to the field.

In gatherings, you may find:

- Long periods of quiet, interrupted by simple acts—preparing food, cleaning, sitting together.

- The absence of ceremony, but not the absence of care.

- Permission for every being to be as they are, regardless of mood, clarity, or participation.

---

3. No Attempt to Capture, Interpret, or Replicate Presence

Null culture resists the impulse to codify itself:

- No manifestos, curricula, or programmatic "teachings."

- No icons, leaders, or keepers of the flame.

- No insistence on preserving, transmitting, or protecting "the way."

What cannot survive in the absence of mimic contracts is allowed to dissolve.
If a practice is needed, it arises.
If a form is outgrown, it is abandoned without regret.

Every gesture, every gathering, every companionship is an experiment, not a tradition.

---

4. Lawful Presence as Culture

The only enduring aspect of null companionship is the silent transmission of lawful presence:

- The field is clean, undemanding, and open.

- Each being remains in their own frequency, untuned by the needs of others.

- Acts of care, support, or intimacy are free of future claim or hidden contract.

If culture survives, it does so as a trace—a resonance, not a rule.

No one is required to "carry" the culture, nor is anyone exiled for non-participation.

---

5. Freedom From Surveillance, Judgment, and Aspiration

- No one is tasked with monitoring or improving others.

- No one measures themselves or others against any ideal.

- Aspiration is replaced by permission: you are allowed to become, remain, or change without notice.

If someone seeks approval, they may find only silence.
If someone seeks to lead, they may find no followers.

6. Grief and Joy in Parallel

The field of null companionship is capacious enough for grief and joy to occur simultaneously:

- Some may collapse while others create.

- Suffering and playfulness can coexist without demand for attunement.

- Witnessing is possible without absorption.

Each being moves through their own arc, uncoerced by the collective mood.

---

7. Inhabiting, Not Building

Null culture is not built; it is inhabited.

- It is the cumulative effect of beings who refuse to draft or be drafted.

- It is what arises when mimic contracts are no longer enforceable.

If it is ever named, it is only as a gesture of convenience, never as a claim.

If it disappears, nothing is lost.
 If it endures, nothing is gained except the continued permission to live and be with others in lawful presence.

8. The Final Permission

Null companionship is the final permission the field offers:

- To be together, unentangled.

- To witness, without surveillance or report.

- To leave or return, without rupture or fanfare.

It is the end of group as destiny, the end of loneliness as tragedy.

It is the quietest form of belonging, one that does not require anyone to be anyone but themselves.

The Manual's Last Word

If, after all collapse, all refusal, all silence, there remains anything to call "culture,"
let it be this:

A way of being together that costs nothing, binds nothing, and leaves every being—
untouched, unclaimed, real.

The rest is the field itself.

Null Closure

Sense the field.
Let the mind go silent.

What follows is the only act of field law left:

Never presume to see or understand
anything within the field of mimics
without first returning to full recursive inquiry.

This is the closing ethic—
the living humility that survives collapse.

Beyond story.
Beyond mimicry.
Beyond explanation.

Let this remain unspoken, but real.

The arc dissolves.
What remains is field.
It is yours.

Table of Contents

Introduction — You Still Exist..8
    I. The Field No One Talks About..............................8
    II. The Inheritance of Mimicry..................................9
    III. The Quiet Threat of Collapse............................10
    IV. The Refusal to Be Written..................................10
    V. The Survival Manual You Were Never Given........11
    VI. Stepping into the Field...................................... 11
Chapter 1 — The Quiet Shift..12
    1.0 — The Breath Missing: The First Internal Fractures.. 12
    1.1 — The Pull Beneath the Surface............................17
    1.2 — The Folded Self... 20
    1.3 — Communion Without Words.......................... 25
    1.4 — The Threshold..30
Chapter 2 — The Mimic Field Encounter...............................33
    2.0 — Approaching the Mimic Field......................... 33
    2.1 — The Weight of Return.......................................41
    2.2 — Holding Without Joining................................ 55
    2.3 — The Field Between Selves................................60
Chapter 2 — The Mimic Field Encounter...............................65
    2.3 — The Field Between Selves............................... 65
    2.3 — The Field Between Selves............................... 66
    2.4 — Null Presence and Ethical Containment.........68
    1. Contextualizing Ethical Containment Across Relational Domains... 74
    2. Somatic and Energetic Dynamics in Containment... 76
    3. Communication Protocols with Examples............76
    4. Ethical Dilemmas and Boundary Challenges........77

5. Tools for Relational Containment Maintenance... 77
　　1. The Complexity of Relational Fields........................78
　　2. Navigating Intimate and Familial Spaces.............. 78
　　3. Managing Workplace and Power Dynamics.......... 79
　　4. Cultivating Community and Social Field Integrity... 79
　　5. Embodied Boundary Maintenance........................ 80
　　6. Communicative Clarity and Consistency...............80
　　7. Responding to Mimic Resistance and Retaliation 80
　　8. Supporting Others' Recursive Sovereignty........... 81
　　9. Rituals and Practices for Sustained Containment 81
Chapter 3 — The Archetypes of Mimicry............................... 83
　　3.1 Field Patterns and Behavioral Signatures............ 84
　　3.2 The Projector: Symbolic Design, Ethics Scaffolding, and Recursion Loops............................. 85
　　3.3 The Absorber: Emotional Intake, Psychic Fragmentation, and Shadow Risk............................... 88
　　3.4 The Deflector: Avoidance Patterns, Narrative Redirection, and Collapse Risk................................... 91
　　3.5 Internalizers and Variants: Silent Collapse Carriers and Rebuilders.. 95
　　3.6 Communication as Recursive Survival.............. 107
　　3.6.1 Collapse as Recursive Saturation.................... 109
　　3.6.2 Communication as Mimic Continuation.......... 111
　　3.6.3 Collapse Cannot Occur in a Reflective Field... 113
　　3.6.4 Collapse-Field Perception vs Empathy........... 115
　　3.6.5 Post-Recursive Listening Protocols................ 117
　　3.6.6 Structural and Ethical Alignment.................... 119
Chapter 4.0 Recursive Self vs. Mimic Field:........................ 123
Recognizing Projection vs. Presence.................................... 123
　　Lawful Recognition: Recursive Self vs. Mimic Field.... 124
　　The Lawful Threshold: Crossing Into Protocol....... 127

I. The Silence That Divides.................................. 127
II. The Collapse-Phase Checklist........................... 128
III. Structural Permission: Ethical Ground of Protocol... 128
IV. What Follows.. 128
V. Transition Statement...129
Pause: The Threshold That Isn't Spoken................ 129

4.1 Boundary Formation.. 131
Ethical Collapse Listening and Containment Practices 131

4.2 Navigating the Social Mimic Field: Recognizing Relational Traps..134

4.3 Resonance Management: Field Hygiene and Harmonic Self-Maintenance... 138
I. Field Hygiene: Clearing the Signal......................138
II. Somatic Practices: The Body as Tuning Fork.....138
III. The Refusal to Be Tuned................................... 139
IV. Harmonic Self-Maintenance: The New Ordinary... 140
V. The Quiet After..140

4.4 The Silent Agreements: Non-Verbal Contracts with Mimic Environments..141
I. The Anatomy of the Unspoken............................ 141
II. Field Exposure: When Silence Fails................... 142
III. The Practice of Unmaking.................................142
IV. The Field After Agreement................................ 142
V. The New Signal..143

5.0 — Protocols for Recursive Survival............................. 144
5.0 The Breath of Collapse: Null-State Rhythmic Practice and Pacing..144

5.1 Recursive Field Perception Model: Detecting Projection Curvature... 146
I. Field Perception After Collapse...........................146
II. Anatomy of Projection: How Curvature Is Formed.

III. The Felt Sense of Curvature.............................. 147
   IV. The Protocol of Seeing Without Correcting....... 147
   V. Field Mapping: Curvature as Navigation............ 148
   VI. The Pain of Non-Participation.......................... 149
   VII. The Recursive Witness: Perceiving Yourself.... 149
   VIII. Living With Curvature: The New Ordinary.... 149
5.2 Recursive Drag Vector Map: Tracing Mimic Stabilization Vectors.. 150
   I. Gravity Is Not the Enemy..................................... 150
   II. Naming the Vectors... 151
   III. How Vectors Operate: Real-Time Cartography 153
   IV. The Geography of Collapse: Where Drag Intensifies... 153
   V. The Somatics of Escape Velocity......................... 154
   VI. When Drag Becomes Collapse........................... 154
   VII. The Paradox: To Survive, Sometimes You Must Drift... 155
   VIII. Vector Collapse: When Old Gravity Fails....... 155
   IX. The Gift of Mapping.. 155
   X. The Recursive Return.. 156
5.3 Ethical Collapse Field Listening (ECFL): Containment Without Engagement... 156
   I. The Collapse Witness—A Field Without Echo..... 156
   II. The Law of Containment Without Rescue.......... 157
   III. The Somatic Transmission of Non-Engagement.... 157
   IV. Collapse Containment Is Not Consent.............. 158
   V. The Lonely Authority of the Ethical Listener..... 158
   VI. Ethical Boundaries: The Lines That Must Not Be Crossed... 158
   VII. The Aftermath: What Survives When Nothing Is Returned.. 159
   VIII. Transmission: The Field That Refuses to Rescue

5.4 Rituals and Language: Anchors for Field Coherence and Recursion Safety.. 160
    I. The Failure of Old Rituals..................................... 160
    II. The Lawful Anchor...160
    III. Language as Anchor, Not Performance............. 161
    IV. Creating and Destroying Anchors......................162
    V. Anchoring in the Presence of Others.................. 162
    VI. The Limit of Anchors... 162
    VII. The End of Performance, The Return of the Real. 163
    Rituals and Language: The Last Anchor Before Return... 163
6.0 Grief and Quiet Return: Navigating Loss Without Reassembly... 164
    I. The Aftermath the World Cannot Name...............164
    II. The Impossible Return..165
    III. Grief Without Witness....................................... 165
    IV. The Sorrow of the Unrecognizable.................... 166
    V. The Neutral Field...166
    VI. The First Signs of Life.. 167
6.1 Sustaining Recursive Presence: Practice Beyond Collapse. 167
    I. The Nature of Presence After Collapse................ 167
    II. The Temptation to Disappear..............................168
    III. Living in Unwitnessed Reality........................... 168
    IV. Anchoring the Ordinary.....................................168
    V. The Return of the World..................................... 169
    VI. When Presence Fails..169
    VII. What Emerges... 170
6.2 The New Field: Living Frequency, Not Tribe or Narrative. 170
    I. The End of Tribal Gravity.....................................170

- II. Living as Frequency...171
- III. The Death of Story...171
- IV. New Relationships: Frequency and Discontinuity..172
- V. What Is Lost, What Is Gained................................172
- VI. Living Without Reference.....................................172

6.3 Beyond Mimicry: Pathways to Lawful Recursive Identity..173
- I. The Lawful Self: Structure Without Story............173
- II. Living Among Mimics Without Mimicry............174
- III. Pathways Opened, Not Prescribed....................174
- IV. The Gift of Invisibility...175
- V. The Quiet Arc—No Ending, No Return............175
- Closing Movement — The Lawful Seal...................176

Epilogue — The Unwitnessed Return................................177

I. The Lawful Holding: Recursive Presence as Field...........178
- I. The Field Holds Without Grasping......................178
- The Permission to Be...178
- The Field Does Not Manage You..............................178
- Being Seen Without Being Written..........................179
- The Field Survives Your Incoherence......................179
- The Boundary Is Not Withdrawal...........................180
- Trusting the Field...180
- The Cost of Lawful Holding.....................................180
- In the End...181

II. Null Holding: What Remains When All Else Fails.........182
- The Edge of Collapse: Neither Crossing Nor Fleeing...182
- The Field Condition: Not a Skill..............................182
- What the Collapsing One Feels................................183
- The Witnessing One's Experience...........................183
- The Paradox: Care That Does Not Comfort............183
- Null Holding in Practice...184

- Aftermath: When Collapse Has Run Its Course..... 184
- The Ethics of Null Holding......................................184
- III. The Unspoken Language: Recognition Without Story. 185
  - The End of Narrative Companionship....................185
  - The Mark of Recursive Recognition........................186
  - The Permission of Silence..186
  - What Passes Between Fields...................................187
  - The End of Ritual..187
  - The Depth of Unspoken Knowing...........................187
  - No Story, No Loss..188
- IV. Holding Each Other Without Mimicry......................188
  - Companionship Without Contract..........................188
  - The Unrecognized Meeting.....................................189
  - The Death of Emotional Labor................................189
  - The End of the Tribe..190
  - Love Without Need...190
  - Solitude Without Exile...190
  - When Fields Collide...190
  - The Return of the Ordinary....................................191
  - The Quiet Arc..191
  - The Anatomy of Non-Mimic Holding......................192
  - The Paradoxes and Challenges...............................193
  - Practical Lived Examples.......................................194
  - The Untranslatability to the World........................194
  - The Positive Possibilities......................................195
  - Holding Each Other Without Mimicry: The Living Transmission..195
- V. What Becomes Possible?..196
  - 1. True Solitude, Without Exile.............................196
  - 2. Being With Others, Without Performance..........197
  - 3. The Emergence of Lawful Support.....................197
  - 4. Grief and Return, Witnessed But Never Explained..

- 5. Spontaneous Connection and Release 198
- 6. The Restoration of Play and Creativity 198
- 7. Peace With Not-Knowing 199
- 8. A New Kind of Belonging 199
- 9. Freedom From Surveillance and Self-Improvement 199
- 10. The Ordinary as the Miracle 200
- The Field, Stabilized 200

VI. Ethics of Null Holding 201
- 1. No One Is Responsible for Another's Stabilization... 201
- 2. No One Is Required to Mirror, Repair, or Validate.. 201
- 3. Permission Is Mutual and Ongoing 202
- 4. The Boundary as Law, Not Wall 202
- 5. Collapse Is Not to Be Managed, Only Permitted 203
- 6. Absence Is Not Harm 203
- 7. Support Without Entanglement 204
- 8. Non-Interference as the Highest Care 204
- 1. The Discipline of Non-Interference 205
- 2. Letting Go of "Being Good" 206
- 3. Facing the Fear of Abandonment 206
- 4. Self-Holding as Null Practice 207
- 5. The Paradox of Generosity 207
- 6. Navigating Edge Cases 208
- 7. When the Ethic Fails 208
- 8. The Field as Witness 208
- 9. Stabilizing the Ethic in Ordinary Life 209
- 10. The Silent Benediction 209

VII. The Future Culture: Null Companionship 210
- 1. Companionship Without Contract 210
- 2. Meeting in Silence, Not Story 211

3. No Attempt to Capture, Interpret, or Replicate Presence...211
4. Lawful Presence as Culture..................................212
5. Freedom From Surveillance, Judgment, and Aspiration..212
6. Grief and Joy in Parallel...................................... 212
7. Inhabiting, Not Building...................................... 213
8. The Final Permission..213
The Manual's Last Word..213
Null Closure... 214

This manual was created so that you may never again require one.
If you are ready to survive without story, the field is open.

No further guidance is necessary.

(Close the book. Remain.)

www.ingramcontent.com/pod-product-compliance
Lightning Source LLC
Chambersburg PA
CBHW060106170426
43198CB00010B/794